State Financial Incentives to Industry

State Financial Incentives to Industry

Daryl A. Hellman
Northeastern University

Gregory H. Wassall
University of Hartford

Laurence H. Falk
Rutgers University

Lexington Books
D.C. Heath and Company
Lexington, Massachusetts
Toronto

Library of Congress Cataloging in Publication Data

Hellman, Daryl A
 State financial incentives to industry.

 Bibliography: p.
 Includes index.
 1. Industrial promotion—United States—States. 2. Industrial development bonds—United States—States. I. Wassall, Gregory H., joint author. II. Falk, Laurence H., joint author. III. Title.
HC110.I53H45 338.973 75-25327
ISBN 0-669-00221-6

Published simultaneously in Canada

Printed in the United States of America

International Standard Book Number: 0-669-00221-6

Library of Congress Catalog Card Number: 75-25327

Contents

List of Tables

Preface

This book is an attempt to clarify the role of state industrial incentive programs and their influence on the investment and location decisions of firms. The three authors began a joint investigation of this subject under a grant from the New Jersey Department of Labor, Division of Economic Development. We are deeply grateful for this assistance.

Our original charge was to examine incentive programs in the Northeast to determine their effectiveness and their relationship to New Jersey's economy. In the spirit of friendly competitors, officials of the states of Connecticut, Delaware, Kentucky, Maryland, Massachusetts, New York, Ohio, and Pennsylvania kindly provided us with descriptions of their programs.

We are indebted to William J. Stober of the University of Kentucky and Matityahu Marcus of Rutgers University for their counsel in early phases of this study. Special thanks go to Peter D. Loeb of Rutgers University-Newark, our former collaborator and co-conspirator. At various phases of this study, Alan Ringquist, Herb Eskowitz, Eileen Meeks, and William O'Grady provided capable research assistance. Irene Gendrone kindly provided editorial assistance. The manuscript was expertly typed by Mary Juliano and Alec Cheloff.

Finally, we are grateful to the Atlantic Economic Society and the University of Rhode Island, respectively, for permission to use the following material: Daryl Hellman, L.H. Falk, and Gregory H. Wassall, "Loan Guarantees as Location Incentives: An Empirical Evaluation of the Connecticut Program," *Atlantic Economic Journal* 3 (1975): 53-60, and Daryl Hellman, Gregory H. Wassall, and Herb Eskowitz, "The Role of Statewide Industrial Incentive Programs in the New England Economy," *New England Journal of Business and Economics* 7 (1975): 10-29.

1 Introduction

State financial incentives to industry enjoy a long and somewhat colorful history. "Deals" existed long before 1936, although that year marks the beginning of formal, legal state financial incentive programs designed to encourage industrial development. It is not surprising that the first program was in Mississippi—and at the end of the Great Depression. The other southern states followed suit, and eventually most of the fifty states, plus Puerto Rico, had enacted some form of industrial inducement program. The programs varied in scope, in expense to the state, and in effectiveness in luring industry. In part this was due to differences in program design, in part to the aggressiveness of the state in promoting its inducement package.

Initially, some observers argued that state financial incentive programs would not last. The programs, they pointed out, would ultimately deteriorate into useless tax giveaways. Introduction of programs would only cause other states to reciprocate, with the net result that industry locations would be unaffected by the lures, and the financial structures of the states would be seriously and unnecessarily impaired.

While this prediciton may eventually be true, industrial inducement programs have been with us for two generations. Partly, this may be because much of the tax "giveaway" has been an erosion of the federal, not the inducement-granting state's tax base. Industrial revenue bonds and industrial development bank mortgages are attractive to industry largely because of a federal tax exemption. Thus the state employing the bonds or mortgages enjoys most of the benefits while the federal government incurs most of the costs. The states can afford to be myopic.

The other reason that inducement programs are still very much with us is that there is some amount of disagreement, if not confusion, concerning how they work. While a good deal has been written by both academics and practitioners concerning industrial inducement programs, a comprehensive treatment, which describes the programs and examines and compares their effectiveness and im-

1

pact both theoretically and empirically, has not been made. We hope this book will provide, at least in part, the missing information that is required for intelligent decision making.

We do not attempt a detailed review of the literature, although we provide an extensive bibliography, which includes references pertaining to state financial incentives as well as to regional development in general. Reference to some of the writing is made within the text, but a systematic review of previous contributions in the field is not provided. Rather than focus on the development of the literature, we focus on the development and impact of the various programs.

We begin in Chapter 2 with a description of the various state financial incentive programs and trace the history of each program as it developed in the United States. Data concerning the relative magnitudes of the programs are included, as well as data on program inception by states. Appendix A contains a useful summary of financial incentive programs by state.

In Chapter 3 we begin our analysis of the effectiveness of industrial incentives by developing a theoretical model of firm behavior and using it to estimate the value of various types of incentive programs to recipient firms. Program efficiency, measured by savings to the firm per dollar of program cost, is determined and compared for different types of programs. Characteristics of programs that make financial incentives more or less attractive are identified. Based on the theoretical model that is developed, the potential of financial incentives to alter the location decision of firms is assessed.

With the theoretical discussion as background, we begin an empirical examination of the impact of industrial incentives on firm location in Chapter 4. We focus on the impact of financial incentives on state investment activity. The focus is a macroeconomic one in the sense that the prime concern is determining the amount by which state investment has been affected by an inducement program.

Three prototype programs are evaluated in Chapter 4: the Connecticut loan guarantee program, the Pennsylvania loan program, and the Kentucky industrial revenue bond program. State investment functions are developed that permit measurement of the impact of an inducement program on investment activity in the state. Estimates of the investment functions, using time series data for each state, permit statistical hypothesis testing concerning the effectiveness of the various programs. They also provide the basis for a cost-benefit analysis of each of the three programs. Benefits to the inducement-granting state, measured by total income created, are compared to costs, measured by total income foregone. Benefit-cost ratios for the three programs are compared.

The final section of Chapter 4 deals with a broader issue: the impact of successful inducement programs on neighboring states. Does an inducement program that increases state investment do so at the expense of investment in a nearby state that does not offer inducements or that has a less attractive inducement package? To answer the question we examine the impact of the Pennsylvania loan program on its neighbor, New Jersey. Throughout the chapter, various methodological problems are addressed.

Chapter 5 provides a microeconomic analysis of incentive programs. The focus is on the industrial composition of participating investment. Characteristics of firms that participated in an industrial revenue bond program are evaluated with respect to area development potential. Employment generated by participating firms is examined, as well as characteristics relevant to long-term growth and ability to solve area unemployment problems. The geographic distribution of participating firms is compared with the geographic distribution of growth and employment problems. The analysis is restricted to Massachusetts.

The final chapter summarizes the findings of each of the previous chapters. Based on the conclusions presented there, recommendations for state, as well as national, policy concerning state financial incentives are provided. We hope that the points made and questions raised in the chapter are of interest not only to academics concerned with regional development and public finance but also to practitioners working in public or private agencies concerned with state and regional economic development.

2

The History and Practice of Statewide Industrial Incentives

Since states have developed a wide variety of programs to attract industry, it is important to create a working definition of state incentive programs before discussing the history and practice of these programs. In this study, two criteria must be met: the program must be state authorized, and it must provide a subsidy to recipient firms from public funds. These criteria exclude federal subsidy programs such as Area Redevelopment Act and Economic Development Act loans, and state programs of a nonsubsidy nature, such as advertising and information services to industry. Business Development Corporations, often cataloged in surveys of state incentives to industry, are also excluded. Although they are authorized by a state charter, funds that they provide to industry are solely from private sources.

Most clearly complying to the above criteria are loan and loan guarantee (or mortgage insurance) programs, which are state authorized and state run and utilize state funds to make direct loans or to insure private loans against default. Tax concessions require authorization by state legislation. The implicit subsidy is borne by state or local government, depending on the tax. Exemption from the local property tax is the most heavily used concession.

The most difficult to justify as a state subsidy is industrial development bond financing. It is usually, but not necessarily, preceded by state legislation empowering either state or (more commonly) local authorities to issue tax-exempt bonds to finance industrial development. The bonds are of the general obligation or revenue type. Although the credit of the state or municipality backs general obligation bond issues, with either type of bond the cost of the subsidy is borne primarily by the federal government. Because of the central role industrial bond financing has played, we will treat it here as a state incentive.

The rest of this chapter is devoted to an examination of the history and use of the state industrial incentives identified above.

Industrial Development Bond Programs

The use of municipal bonding power to finance industrial development has had a lengthier history than most other industrial inducements. Before pursuing it, the distinction among municipal bonds used for this purpose should be clarified. An *industrial development bond* (IDB) is defined as a municipal bond used to finance an industrial project. A *revenue bond* is a municipal bond whose repayment is tied to the revenues expected from a project financed by the bond issue. A *general obligation bond* is a municipal bond whose repayment is the obligation of the municipal entity that issued it. Revenue and general obligation bonds can be and have been used to finance industrial development projects.

Revenue bonds came into existence in the early 1890s. From the colonial period to that time, projects now commonly financed by revenue bonds were often financed by obligations backed by the full faith and credit of the state. Many of these issues defaulted, causing a number of states to pass laws prohibiting further pledging of state or local credit for such projects.

The first municipal revenue bonds were issued by Spokane, Washington, in the 1890s to finance its waterworks.[1] The state of Washington soon authorized the issuance of these bonds, and other states later followed suit. By the 1920s, revenue bonds were widely used to finance construction of utilities, bridges, and other revenue-producing but essentially public projects.

The use of municipal bonds to finance industrial projects began in 1936 in Mississippi with the creation of the state's Balance Agriculture With Industry program.[2] The IDBs that financed this program were of the general obligation type. Principally because revenue bonds did not require the backing of the issuing governmental entity, they eventually became more widely used than general obligation bonds for industrial development financing. Ironically, Mississippi was one of the few states to continue using general obligation bond financing to any degree.[3]

IDB financing did not catch on immediately. Between 1936 and 1948 only Mississippi authorized the use of IDBs, and it did not use them very extensively. By 1963 twenty-five additional states had also authorized their use. As of May 1973, forty-six states had IDB financing programs.[4] As can be seen in Table 2-1, the use of IDBs rose steadily from the 1950s to 1968. The volume of issues in 1968

($1.6 billion) was over 200 times that of 1957 and comprised 10 percent of all municipal bond offerings.[5] (The period 1963-1968 may be considered the heyday of IDB financing because of legal rulings, which will be examined later.)

Growth in bond financing was due not only to its adoption by an increasing number of states, but also because states often bestowed bond-issuing power on substate governments and nonprofit agencies as well. Mississippi allowed project financing by substate governments and industrial development agencies created by them from 1936.[6] The second state to do so was Kentucky in 1958. This trend also caught on quickly; by 1960, thirteen states had granted their municipalities such powers. This number rose to thirty-eight by October 1969 and to forty-three by May 1973.[7]

Unlike other forms of industrial aid financing, IDBs have remained primarily a device used by southern states. During the 1959-1969 period when the majority of IDBs were floated, six southern states (Alabama, Arkansas, Georgia, Kentucky, Mississippi, and Tennessee) accounted for 87 percent of all issues and 60 percent of the dollar volume of IDBs.[8]

Legal rulings, opinions, and legislation have greatly affected the growth and ultimate demise of the IDB. The lag between the creation of the IDB and heavy use of it was caused in part by uncertainty of its legality and ultimate effects. As early as 1951 the Investment Bankers' Association publicly stated its opposition to IDB financing. Other organizations (the Advisory Commission on Intergovernmental Relations in 1959 and the Municipal Forum of New York in 1965) were critical of IDB financing in reports, although they did not condemn the practice.

Most academics, with the exception of John Moes, had a low opinion of IDB financing.[9] Several authors opined (some in response to Moes) that only marginal firms were attracted by IDBs and that such firms would vacate their plants as soon as the subsidy expired.[10]

The constitutionality of Mississippi's IDB program was upheld by the U.S. Supreme Court in 1938.[11] However, courts in Idaho, Nebraska, and Florida rejected revenue bond financing, usually on the ground that their state constitutions prohibit the lending of public funds for private use. In many states, a constitutional amendment was necessary to permit IDB financing.

In such an environment the development of a broad market for

Table 2-1
Annual Volume of Industrial Development Bond Financing
(Millions of Dollars)

Year	IBA-SIA Estimates	ACIR Estimates	ABRC Estimates	Average Size of Bond Issue[a]	Estimates (IBA-SIA) by Type of Issuer					
					State	County	Municipality	Special District	Statutory Authority	School District
1974	493	$	$	$1.80	$ 23	$ 90	$169	$ 2	$208	$0
1973	573			2.05	11	161	143	8	251	0
1972	296			2.37	14	51	103	4	124	0
1971	207			1.57	1	49	73	0	75	0
1970	115			1.40	4	37	41	0	28	0
1969	51			0.75	0	16	12	2	18	0
1968	1,606		1,806.20	8.52	10	601	581	31	383	0
1967	1,315		1,387.65	6.09	133	188	548	4	443	0
1966	504		629.90	2.56	6	47	245	4	208	0
1965	216.16		295.39	1.64	2	14.34	78.31	1.94	119.58	0
1964	192.64		296.11	1.55	0	16.15	130.53	3.40	42.07	0.48
1963	119.78		189.69	1.33	0	5.46	87.30	1.70	25.15	0.17

Year									
1962	65.93	87.84	109.70	0.83	0	1.83	28.27	4.06	30.26	1.51
1961	41.27	83.47	106.88	0.96	0	4.07	32.44	1.45	2.12	1.19
1960	41.02	103.02	78.77	0.64	0	6.93	24.35	9.35	0.40	0
1959	17.99	45.54	32.38	0.37	17	2.73	12.67	2.56	0	0
1958	25.84	17.50	33.46	0.48	0	1.60	5.47	3.76	15.00	0
1957	7.08	19.84		0.24	0	1.30	5.00	0.75	0.03	0
1956		8.23		0.28						
1955		7.28								
1954	5.02									
1953	5.27									
1952	7.60									
1951	9.62									
Pre-1951	7.25									

[a]Data for years 1969-1974 from IBA-SIA; data for years 1956-1968 from ABRC, *Industrial Development Financing*.

Sources: Investment Bankers' Association and (since February 1972) Securities Industry Association, *Municipal Statistical Bulletin*, Nos. 1-68; Advisory Commission on Intergovernmental Relations, *Industrial Development Bond Financing* (Washington, D.C., 1963), p. 55. Alabama Business Research Council, *Industrial Development Financing: Business and Community Experience and Opinions* (1970), p. 20.

Note: All three sets of estimates are subject to underreporting. IBA-SIA and ACIR estimates exclude some issues sold locally and neither reported to IBA-SIA or state agencies nor nationally advertised. ABRC estimates include data from state agencies in the six most active states (Alabama, Arkansas, Georgia, Kentucky, Mississippi, Tennessee) but are otherwise subject to the same deficiencies.

IDB buyers was difficult. Until 1960, few investment houses under-wrote them, and large financial institutions avoided them in their portfolios. Members of the community in which the plant was to be located were often expected to absorb the bond issue.

One factor that led to a wider market for IDBs was their increasing use by large, nationally known firms. This provided assurance to investors in these bonds, particularly revenue bonds, that their risk was not great and broadened the market of potential investors. Whether increased use of IDB financing by large firms was caused by greater aggressiveness by states and municipalities or was a response by firms to rising interest rates throughout the late 1950s is not clear.

A second factor was clarification by the Internal Revenue Service of the status of tax-exempt IDB financing. It was clear that obligations of states and their political subdivisions were exempt from taxation. A 1954 ruling certified that this privilege extended to revenue bonds and bonds of municipally owned corporations regardless of the purpose of the bond issue.[12] A 1957 ruling stated that bonds issued by an industrial development board authorized by a state would be considered an issue by a political subdivision of the state and therefore tax exempt.[13]

The strongest positive impetus was provided in a 1963 ruling that allowed nonprofit corporations, under certain specified circumstances, to issue tax-exempt industrial bonds.[14] This enabled municipalities to utilize IDB financing even though their states might not have granted legislative authorization. The rapid growth of IDB financing from 1963 to 1969 was a consequence of this ruling.

The rapid reduction in IDB financing from 1969 reflects the reaction to two governmental actions that occurred in 1968. The first, and probably most important, was contained in an amendment to the Revenue and Expenditure Control Act of 1968 that limited federal income tax exemption on the interest payments of IDBs to those issues of $1 million or less.[15] After considerable lobbying by nonfederal governmental bodies, Congress modified this law. Currently, a state or local government or a nonprofit development corporation may (1) provide a tax-exempt IDB issue up to $1 million to a firm with no restriction on capital spending or (2) provide a tax-exempt IDB issue up to $5 million with the restriction that the recipient firm is limited to a capital spending program of no more than $5 million in any one location within the county for a period of three years before and three years after the issue.[16] This legislation also prohibited corporations and their officers from acquiring IDBs issued to finance their own plant. The importance of the limitation can be seen by noting that the average amount of an IDB issue in 1968 was $8.5 million, and many issues were considerably larger than this.

The second blow dealt IDB financing in 1969 was an administrative ruling by the Securities and Exchange Commission requiring industrial revenue bond issues more than $300,000 to be registered with the SEC and to be subject to all regulations applicable to issues of a corporate security. General obligation industrial bonds were not subject to these registration requirements. Also, two types of revenue bond issues were exempt from this requirement: (1) if the project is located in a state where the lessee is incorporated and the bond purchasers are residents of that state, and (2) if the bonds are offered to a limited number of "knowledgeable" investors.

The effect of the removal of the tax-exempt privilege on issues above a certain size is obvious. The SEC registration requirement compounds difficulties involved in issuing tax-exempt revenue bonds because registration costs do not increase in proportion to size of issue and are most burdensome in the tax-exempt range.[a]

To alleviate the difficulty in floating tax-exempt revenue bonds, Congress enacted in 1970 a provision that IDB issues which satisfy tax-exemption requirements are also exempt from SEC registration requirements. The data in Table 2-1 show that the principal constraint upon IDB financing has been removal of the tax-exempt status of large issues, and not SEC requirements. Aggregate bond issues are still substantially below 1968 levels.

Because of the variations in IDB financing practices, it is impossible to specify a typical bond transaction. As noted, only thirteen states utilize general obligation bonds for industrial financing but use of revenue bonds has spread to forty-six.[17] In addition, most IDB financing occurs at the local level. In only five states is there an authority at the state level empowered to issue exempt bonds for industrial development projects. In thirty-five states the municipality, county, or other local governmental unit is empowered to issue IDBs; local nonprofit development corporations have been set up

---

[a] Pennsylvania attempted to minimize adverse effects of these rulings when it instituted its "industrial mortgage" program in 1970. This program consisted of private placements of revenue bond issues with one or a few buyers, typically banks. SEC registration requirements were thus avoided (while they remained in existence), and costs of a public bond offering were avoided. It corresponds to a typical revenue bond issue in other respects.

for this purpose in fourteen states. In a number of states, more than one of these financing sources is operative.

The typical bond-financed plant is leased from the state or local government or nonprofit development corporation to the tenant; however, some states provide for outright ownership of the facility by the tenant.[18] Even when ownership is permissible, it can be financially advantageous to the tenant firm to lease rather than own. In many states, the tenant is allowed to purchase the leased property for a nominal amount when the bonds are paid off. Such an option was usually incorporated in lease arrangements. The Internal Revenue Service argued that such an arrangement may constitute financing rather than leasing and the lessee should be compelled to deduct depreciation instead of lease payments from income. The portion of lease payments constituting repayment of bond interest is deductible, however.[19]

The bond flotation typically covers costs of land acquisition and plant construction. One of several "unpublished restrictions" clarifying Revenue Ruling 63-20 stated that equipment for any otherwise eligible industrial project cannot be included in project cost underwritten by revenue bond financing.[20] Nevertheless, more than half the states that engage in IDB financing specify that relevant machinery and equipment may be included as part of project cost financed by the bonds.

Although bond financing was originally considered a vehicle for avoiding property taxes, currently most state laws dictate that the project occupant must include a payment in lieu of taxes as part of the lease payments or, in some cases, must pay property taxes directly. In some states, however, particularly in the South, tax payments are still not required. Fourteen states currently exempt IDB-financed projects from property taxation. Exemption generally coincides with public ownership of the project.

Like other financial incentive programs, geographical constraints on IDB financing exist in a few states. These normally take the form of limiting exempt financing to depressed or high unemployment areas or to specific areas targeted for industrial development; however, this is the exception rather than the rule.

Loan and Loan Guarantee Programs

An important source of funds for inducement purposes has been direct loans or state guarantees of private loans. All states with these programs—except California, Hawaii, and Mississippi—have created a state-level industrial finance or industrial development authority to administer them.

The history of these programs is briefer than that of IDB financing. New Hampshire authorized the first state industrial finance authority in 1955; by 1959, five more states had authorized programs. This number grew to fifteen in 1963 and to twenty-two in 1973. States authorizing loan programs grew from three to fourteen to sixteen in these years, and those authorizing loan guarantee programs grew from four to seven to thirteen in the same years.[21]

Loan and loan guarantee programs are most heavily used in the Northeast. Gooding refers to these two incentives as the North's weapons in the "war between the states" for new industry.[22] Of nine northeastern states, five have authorized loan programs and five have authorized loan guarantee programs. Although only incomplete information exists, it would appear that the most extensive of these programs are also situated in the Northeast. Pennsylvania and New York have the most active loan programs; Connecticut, Maine, Maryland, Rhode Island, and Vermont lead in the amount of loans guaranteed.[b] This is not surprising since these programs have been in existence the longest.

Amounts of money lent under these programs are not as great, on an annual basis, as aggregate bond offerings, even with the current restrictions on revenue bond financing. This conclusion partially reflects the nature of loan programs; only a fraction of total project costs is usually lent. Even Pennsylvania, the state with the most active loan program, finances more industrial projects with its revenue bond and industrial mortgage programs.

Loan Programs

A wide variety of loan programs exists. A small number—about five—are limited in size, and their lending authority is restricted to special situations. The remainder, including the most active loan programs, have much in common.

---

[b] Not all states with programs reported amounts lent or guaranteed in the New York State Department of Commerce survey. Of those that did, Pennsylvania's ($274 million lent through January 1973) and New York's ($74 million lent through October 1973) stand out among loan programs; no other state reported more than $20 million lent. Connecticut, Maine, Maryland, Rhode Island, and Vermont report guaranteeing $29-50 million in loans; no other reporting state had guaranteed more than $15 million.

The state industrial development agency normally lends a specified portion of total project costs on a second mortgage basis. In the most typical form of loan, the state agency contributes 25 to 50 percent of project cost, a local development agency supplies 10 percent, and a financial institution provides the remainder on a first mortgage basis. Duration of the loan is usually ten to twenty years.

In some states limitations are placed on the nature of property covered by the loan and on areas within the state where the project is to be constructed. A number of states limit loan funds to financing of land and buildings. The project tenant in most states is a manufacturing firm, although it may also be a research and development firm or a warehouse.

The incentive, naturally, is the rate of interest the state charges for its proportion of the loan. The local development corporation matches the state's lending rate in most states. Funds for loan programs are acquired by states from either tax-exempt bond issues or by legislative appropriation.[c] Most programs lend at their tax-exempt borrowing rate, or they may add a slight premium. A few programs lend at lower rates. Pennsylvania initiated the use of low interest rates and has maintained a lending rate of 2 percent throughout most of its program's existence.

Loan Guarantee Programs

Loan guarantee programs also offer a reduced lending rate as their principal attraction, the lower rate reflecting the state guarantee. Most loan guarantee programs attempt to operate as a lender of last resort, and they limit their guarantees to firms that cannot obtain funds from conventional sources. (Note that this also applies to a number of loan programs as well.) The cost of guaranteeing the loan is borne primarily by a service charge in the form of an increment to the private lender's rate. This charge is normally one-half to 1 percent of outstanding balances. The lending rate on a typical guaranteed loan is "slightly higher than conventional bank mortgages."[23]

When a loan guarantee program is established, a reserve fund is

---

[c] States that rely on municipal bond issues are generally of the opinion that they must limit their loans to no more than $5 million per project in conformance with industrial bond regulations.

set up to provide for defaults. This fund is usually a very small percentage of the total guarantee authorization. However, the limited information available on losses indicates that they have been very low, and a number of states have had no defaults.

Similar to loan programs, the vast majority of guaranteed loans go to industrial enterprises. Guaranteed loans on plant and land normally have maturities of twenty to twenty-five years, with the state authority insuring up to 90 percent of the loan; a local development corporation provides the rest. Most programs will also guarantee loans on machinery and equipment. The maximum maturity for this loan ranges from seven to fifteen years among states; typically a lower percentage of the loan is guaranteed. Most states set a maximum to the size of a loan for one project. Limitations on maximum loan size range from $1 million to $10 million, with the New England programs having higher loan ceilings than programs elsewhere.

Tax Concessions

Tax concessions are probably the most difficult type of incentive to classify. They have been in existence longer than other incentives, appear in a variety of forms, and are often granted sub rosa and not reported in surveys. Furthermore, the distinction among various types of tax concessions can be cloudy.

The use of tax incentives to industry dates back to America's infancy. In 1791 the state of New Jersey granted a new firm and its employees exemptions from taxes.[24] Although New Jersey rescinded such tax exemptions in 1800, three other states authorized them to attract industry during the nineteenth century.[25]

The difficulty in estimating the extent of tax concessions can be demonstrated with the aid of Table 2-2, which summarizes the results of five surveys of tax concessions. It is clear that not only did the scope of the surveys vary but also the authors had different conceptions of a tax concession. Property tax concessions are the most commonly discussed device when the subject of tax incentives to locating firms is broached. Yet these concessions take several forms. Most commonly, states exempt, for a period of up to ten years, all taxable property of a newly locating enterprise. The number of such states ranges from eight to eleven in these surveys.

(The Morgan study classifies thirteen states with "exemptions" but does not specify which exemptions exclude less than all taxable property classes or less than a full exemption.) The Johnson study additionally identifies fifteen states in which municipalities grant exemptions although they are not legally empowered to do so. The New York State study notes nine states that grant exemptions only in conjunction with a revenue bond issue.[d] Another five states also exempt bond-financed projects, but grant exemptions to other new industry as well. Finally, Moes (1953 data) lists nine states and Bridges (1963 data) lists thirteen states with "tax concessions," but neither identifes the concessions.[26] Their estimates are consistent with those in Table 2-2. As might be expected, the various property tax concessions are located principally in southern and New England states, where other incentives are heavily used as well.

That a state has legislative authority to offer property tax concessions does not necessarily mean that it frequently offers them. Use varies from almost never to granting exemptions to virtually all new industry. Unfortunately only three states (Alabama, Louisiana, and Montana) provide estimates of the value of their exemptions. Morgan estimated the foregone revenue from exemptions granted during the 1958-1961 period in seven states in which they are widely used. This amounted to $167 million.[27] The magnitude of the foregone revenue is more impressive if one realizes that the $167 million represents gross (of taxes) savings to recipients; a comparable figure for the other incentive programs would be gross annual savings in interest costs rather than total amount lent.[e]

Certain types of property tax exemptions are also granted in

---

[d] If they may be called exemptions in the sense used here. In these states, the bond-financed project is exempt from taxation because it is owned by a nonprofit organization (the local development agency), which floated the bond issue.

[e] To cite some rough comparisons: From IBA-SIA data (Table 2-1), we see that $126,121,000 worth of revenue bonds were issued in the 1958-1961 period, compared with a market value of tax-exempt industry estimated to be $1,621,600,000 for the same period. See William E. Morgan, "The Effects of State and Local Tax Inducements on Industrial Location," (dissertation University of Colorado, 1964). The interest savings for the bond issues can be estimated by using Moody's state and local and industrial bond interest rates for the years in question and assuming quarterly payments. Savings in interest payments for the 1958-1961 period are $2,169,000. From Table IX (p. 126) in Morgan, the value of tax exemptions for the seven states noted above for the same time period can be derived. This amount is $40,414,000, or 18.6 times the "value" of the aggregate bond subsidy. Of course, a different number of projects is associated with each figure, and the years of massive revenue bond issues were still to come (although many of these issues would be coupled with a property tax exemption); nevertheless, even a rough comparison shows the relative aggregate importance of tax exemptions as a subsidy to industry. Its relative importance to the individual firm will be explored in Chapter 3.

Table 2-2
Tax Concessions: Results of Five State Surveys

Type of Concession	Survey and Year				
	Johnson (1962)	Morgan (1963)	Gooding (1964)	ACIR (1966)	N.Y. Department of Commerce (1973)
Property Tax					
Exemption	9	13	10	8	10
Sub-rosa exemption	15	*	*	*	*
Exemption with bond financing only	*	*	*	*	9
Exemption: Certain industries only	1	5	5	2	1
Exemption: Certain property classes only	3	*	*	2	3
Rate or assessment reduction or freeze	2	*	2	1	2
Other					
Income tax exemption or credit	*	*	1	8	2
Sales tax exemption or credit	*	*	2	*	3
Accelerated depreciation	*	*	2	*	*
Free Port					
Exemption	4	*	29	*	*
Exemption: Certain industries only	*	*	3	*	*

*Classification not used in that survey.

Sources: William A. Johnson, "Industrial Tax Exemptions: Sound Investment or Foolish Giveaway?" *Proceedings of the 55th Annual Conference of the National Tax Association*, 1962, pp. 433-35; William Edward Morgan, "The Effects of State and Local Tax Inducements on Industrial Location" (Ph.D. diss., University of Colorado, 1964), p. 116; Edwin C. Gooding, "New War Between the States: Part IV," *New England Business Review*, October 1964, pp. 4-5; Advisory Commission on Intergovernmental Relations, *State-Local Taxation and Industrial Location* (Washington, D.C., 1967), pp. 109-10; New York State Department of Commerce, *The Use of Public Funds or Credit in Industrial Location* (Albany, 1974), pp. 8-92.

blanket form to all industry; however, the purpose of these exemptions is usually a mixture of administrative efficiency and encouragement of industrial development. These exemptions almost always apply to some form of personal property.[28] The most common example is the freeport exemption, noted by Gooding's survey, which entitles property stored in one state but destined for shipment to another state to exemption from taxation as inventories. Some states also exempt domestic inventories and various categories of machinery and equipment. Pollution control equipment is a particular favorite.[29] In only two states is no tangible personal property exempt from taxation.[30]

New industry also benefits, in a few states, from reduction in other forms of taxation. These concessions include exemptions of purchases of machinery and equipment for new plants from sales taxation, various forms of credits against income and sales taxes, and accelerated depreciation. Similar incentives designed to stimulate industrial development are often made available to all firms. The general sales tax is usually viewed as a tax on retail sales, and no state taxes raw materials and other components entering into the manufacturing process. Taxation of machines, tools, and equipment is more ambiguous; the study of the Advisory Commission on Intergovernmental Relations notes that these were exempt in seventeen of the forty-three states with a sales tax in 1964.[31] Also common is the use in income tax apportionment formulas of a sales destination factor. To the extent that a firm sells its products out of state (as firms that comprise the economic base of a region supposedly do) its income tax liability within the state is reduced. The ACIR noted that twenty-six of thirty-nine states in 1966 with a corporation income tax used the sales destination factor in determining liability.[32] Less common is preferential treatment granted to assist exploitation of environmental and locational advantages, such as Louisiana's natural gas severance tax rebate.[33]

Summary

Industrial incentives were probably used most heavily by states in the mid-1960s. It is during that period that they attracted the most notoriety. But criticism has subdued, and these programs have by no means died out. More states have established industrial incentive programs than ever before. Loan and loan guarantee programs, in particular, appear to be growing in use.

A general discussion of the various incentives raises as many questions as it answers. In responses to questionnaires, firms consistently rank incentives low when enumerating location determinants, yet states continue to offer incentives. To what extent do they really work? Some incentive programs are used more heavily than others; use of one program may be concentrated in a certain geographic area. Are rational economic decisions by states and firms behind this distribution? Do states administer their programs in a manner that maximizes net benefits? These are some questions to which we turn in following chapters.

3

The Value of Financial Incentives to the Firm: A Model

In this chapter a theoretical model is developed to estimate the cost savings to a representative firm that accepts a financial incentive.[1] Five types of incentives will be analyzed: property tax exemption, investment tax credit, revenue bond, low interest loan, and loan guarantee. Before proceeding to the specific cases an introduction to the model is necessary.

Consider the present value cost to the firm of constructing a new facility. Call this outlay K_o. In a world of perfect certainty, a stream of revenues $R(t)$ and a stream of operating, maintenance, processing, transportation, and other costs $A(t)$ can be attributed to this investment outlay. The firm will choose the outlay that maximizes the present value of its after-tax net revenue stream. In most general terms the present value of the investment can be represented as

$$PV(I) = \int_0^n (1 - T)[R(t) - A(t)]e^{-rt}\, dt - K_o \qquad (3.1)$$

where n = economic life of the investment; T = marginal federal and state income tax rate, that is, $T = T_f + T_s - T_f T_s$ in most states; $R(t)$ = revenue stream; $A(t)$ = cost stream; and r = firm's cost of capital.

This present value will be location specific. Gross revenues and costs normally will vary with location, and the firm will consider alternatives in its attempt to maximize the present value of its investment in a new plant. To simplify the mathematics, it is assumed that the firm pays transportation costs on its finished product and that it cannot influence the geographically invariant price of output, which has a uniformly distributed spatial demand. Thus only costs will vary with location. The costs of some materials, labor, and transportation and state and local taxes can all be expected to vary with location and will be implicit in our model.

The initial outlay K_o may be financed by internal funds, a stock issue, or borrowing. Because interest subsidies represent debt financing at a rate cheaper than that conventionally obtainable, the opportunity cost of financing K_o is measured as the cost of conventional debt.

Choosing one standard method of conventional financing is necessary to enable consistent comparisons among alternative interest subsidy plans to be made. In terms of equilibrium investments at the margin, the choice among debt and equity instruments should not affect potential savings to the firm when conventional and incentive financing are compared. When it is recognized that a firm may not always possess an optimal capital structure and investments not necessarily at the margin are considered, as is the case in this chapter, savings to the firm are sensitive to the method of conventional financing. Thus consistency in comparison of savings to the firm among alternative interest subsidy plans is ensured by choosing debt as the conventional finance standard. It is assumed that the firm is sufficiently large and its projects sufficiently small so that its investment will not affect its credit rating in the debt market.

In estimating savings to the firm from tax subsidies, the problem of consistency among alternative methods of financing does not arise. A tax subsidy does not influence the method of financing. It is assumed that recipients of tax subsidies use debt finance as well; however, it will be seen that, when calculating savings from acceptance of a tax subsidy, the method of finance used is irrelevant.

With the method of finance now made explicit, equation (3.1) can be developed more fully. Because revenues have been assumed not to vary with location, only costs need be examined. Debt finance enables the firm to spread the outlay on the new facility into the future. Letting L represent annual debt repayments, this can be expressed as

$$K_o = \int_0^n L e^{-it}\, dt \tag{3.2}$$

Integrating and solving for L yields

$$L = \frac{K_o i}{1 - e^{-in}}. \tag{3.2a}$$

Tax considerations enter into this model in two important ways:[a] interest and other costs of doing business are tax deductible, and depreciation of the nonland portion of the initial investment is tax

---

[a] During some recent years in the era of state financial incentives, a federal investment tax credit was in effect. To avoid further complexity, the tax credit will be assumed not in effect in the computations in this chapter; however, its implications will be discussed.

deductible. It has been demonstrated that under most circumstances the sum of the years-digits method of depreciation creates a depreciation stream of greatest present value for a given investment.[2] The present value of this depreciation stream per dollar of capital outlay, assuming no salvage value, can be expressed as

$$D(t) = \int_0^n \frac{2(n - t)e^{-rt}}{n^2} \, dt \tag{3.3}$$

Given the above considerations, the cost C of our hypothetical project, in present value, is:

$$C = \int_0^n \left\{ (1 - T)A(t) + \frac{K_o i}{1 - e^{-in}} [1 - T(1 - e^{-in}e^{it})] \right.$$

$$\left. -\rho T K_o \left[\frac{2(n - t)}{n^2} \right] \right\} e^{-rt} \, dt, \tag{3.4}$$

where ρ = proportion of initial project outlay K_o comprised of depreciable capital. It is implicit in the above expression that the depreciable life of the investment and the time of repayment of the debt are the same. This assumption will be relaxed when it becomes empirically relevant to do so. Another simplification can be made by restricting the capital outlay to a value of one dollar. This can be done by dividing equation (3.4) by K_o. Carrying out the required integration yields

$$C^* = (1 - T) \left[A^* + \frac{i(1 - e^{-rn})}{r(1 - e^{-in})} \right] + T \left[\frac{i(e^{-rn} - e^{-in})}{(i - r)(1 - e^{-in})} \right]$$

$$- \frac{2\rho T}{rn} \left[1 - \frac{1 - e^{-rn}}{rn} \right], \tag{3.4a}$$

where C^* and A^* are costs per dollar of capital outlay.

The cost of conventional financing as characterized in equation (3.4a) can now be compared to costs for the same project when financed by various subsidy programs, and the resulting savings can be estimated. These estimates of cost savings are the end product of a number of simplifying assumptions and choices of values for the parameters. Although the savings estimates discussed below are in line with intuitive expectations, information about the ordinal ranking of programs is probably more conclusive and reliable than numerical values of the data themselves.

Tax Subsidies

Two tax incentives are analyzed: property tax exemption, which has had widespread use, and the investment tax credit, which has had limited use. In the analysis, potential savings attainable if the firm made the same investment with and without the subsidy are calculated.[b] In the case of tax incentives it is presumed that the method of financing would not be altered in light of the subsidy.

Property Tax Exemption

Consider the annual property tax payments as grouped with other operating costs in the $A(t)$ term in equations (3.1) and (3.4). Savings to the firm from the exemption can then be computed directly since other operating costs and the method of project financing will not be affected by the subsidy. Thus we have

$$S_{pte}^* = \int_0^n (1 - T)T_p\varepsilon e^{-rt}\, dt, \qquad (3.5)$$

where S_{pte}^* = savings to the firm per dollar outlay resulting from the property tax exemption; T_p = marginal effective property tax rate; and ε = proportion of project subject to property taxation. Integrating equation (5.5) results in

$$S_{pte}^* = (1 - T)T_p\varepsilon\left(\frac{1 - e^{-rn}}{r}\right). \qquad (3.5a)$$

It was noted in Chapter 2 that property tax exemption programs typically take two forms; a ten-year exemption or a "lifetime" exemption implicit in the lease of a publicly owned facility to the firm, the facility having been financed by a revenue bond issue. Analysis of the second form will be postponed until the discussion of revenue bonds.

Besides a subsidy life of ten years the marginal income tax rate will be set at 0.5.[c] Other parameters—the effective tax rate and proportion of the facility subject to taxation—are more difficult to

---

[b] This analysis therefore does not permit the firm to substitute land and capital for labor as the former two inputs are subsidized. In effect, the estimate of savings resulting from the subsidy is a minimum because it accounts for the income but not the substitution effect.

[c] This implies a federal rate of 0.48, a state rate of 0.04, and deductibility of the state tax from the federal. The tax rate of 0.5 will be employed in other calculations in this chapter.

pinpoint. Both these parameters very considerably from state to state. The states that have utilized exemptions most frequently are in the Southeast, with moderate usage in New England as well.[3] Effective property tax rate data obtained in 1966 and 1971 by the U.S. Census of Governments show a range of rates from 0.3 to 3.5 percent for local areas in southeastern states offering tax exemptions to industry, with most concentrated between 0.9 and 1.6. For New England states, the range was 2.3 to 5.3, with values most commonly falling between 2.5 and 3.5.[4] Sales of industrial property are underrepresented in these data. Such sales occur infrequently, and, when they do, it is often difficult or impossible to extract the cash equivalent selling price. However, assessment-sales ratio studies typically reveal that commercial and industrial property are subject to higher effective tax rates than other classes of property.[5] Also, states with property tax classification systems invariably assess industrial property at higher ratios than other classes, such as residential and farm property.[6] These considerations led to choosing 1, 2, and 3 percent as typical effective tax rates for the states and time periods involved.

The proportion of the industrial facility subject to taxation is primarily dependent on the state's personal property tax statutes. Of the states that have offered exemptions, one exempts all personal property but most exempt little or no business personal property.[7] The proportion of value of a typical new industrial facility composed of machinery and equipment is estimated to be 53 percent of costs, although there is likely to be substantial variation about that estimate in actual facilities (see Appendix B). This would suggest that if no personal property were taxed, about 50 percent of the facility would still be subject to taxation. But since virtually all business personal property is taxed, the proportion of taxable property will be set at 0.5, 0.9, and 1.0 in the estimates of savings to the firm from tax exemption.

These estimates are depicted, for various rates of return, in Table 3-1. Savings are reduced for firms that apply a high discount rate in choosing among investments; they also increase linearly in proportion to the property tax rate and percentage of taxable property. Cutting the length of the exemption to five years would reduce its present value by 43 to 34 percent, depending on that firm's rate of return; extending it to the depreciable life of a plant (forty-five years) would increase its present value from 37 to 110 percent. The figures in the table, in terms of percentage of investment costs in a new

Table 3-1
Savings to the Firm: Property Tax Exemption

	$n = 10, \varepsilon = 0.5, T = 0.5$				
			r		
T_p	*0.06*	*0.08*	*0.10*	*0.12*	*0.14*
0.01	0.01840	0.01678	0.01536	0.01413	0.01304
0.02	0.03680	0.03355	0.03072	0.02825	0.02608
0.03	0.05520	0.05033	0.04608	0.04238	0.03913
	$n = 10, \varepsilon = 0.9, T = 0.5$				
			r		
T_p	*0.06*	*0.08*	*0.10*	*0.12*	*0.14*
0.01	0.03312	0.03020	0.02765	0.02543	0.02347
0.02	0.06624	0.06039	0.05530	0.05085	0.04694
0.03	0.09936	0.09059	0.08295	0.07628	0.07042
	$n = 10, \varepsilon = 1.0, T = 0.5$				
			r		
T_p	*0.06*	*0.08*	*0.10*	*0.12*	*0.14*
0.01	0.03680	0.03355	0.03072	0.02825	0.02608
0.02	0.07360	0.06710	0.06144	0.05650	0.05216
0.03	0.11040	0.10065	0.09217	0.08476	0.07824

facility, can best be interpreted in the context of estimates of savings from other incentives and their locational influence. This will be done at relevant points in this chapter. Partial exemptions, exemptions to selected industries, assessment reductions, and tax freezes can all be evaluated using equation (3.5a). The present value of cost savings for such programs will be less to the extent that these programs are partial exemptions.

Investment Tax Credit

Somewhat different in effect is the tax credit. Analyzed below is one that is offered to newly locating industry by New York State. A credit of 1 percent of qualified capital investment is applied against

Table 3-2
Savings to the Firm: Investment Tax Credit
($T_f = 0.48$, $\xi = 0.01$)

ρ	Savings
0.95	0.00494
0.90	0.00468
0.85	0.00442
0.80	0.00416

the corporate franchise or unincorporated business income tax. "Qualified" capital consists of buildings, equipment, and facilities with a useful life of at least four years. The asset guideline life period used by the Internal Revenue Service for manufacturing assets is, for virtually all types of assets, greater than four years.[8] Thus qualified capital in manufacturing may be considered equivalent to depreciable capital.

Since the credit is granted on a one-time basis, future savings need not be discounted. Savings from an investment tax credit may be calculated as

$$S_{itc}^* = (1 - T_f)\xi\rho, \tag{3.6}$$

where S_{itc}^* = savings to the firm per dollar outlay resulting from the investment tax credit, and ξ = the value of the credit stated as the ratio of qualifying capital to total cost. Note that equation (3.6) is valid only if the dollar value of the credit is less than the state corporation income tax liability. Also, the value of the credit is reduced in proportion to the federal corporation income tax rate since the credit reduces state liability, and thus federal deductibility, dollar for dollar.

Calculation of savings per dollar of total outlay is straghtforward. In Appendix B, the most typical value of ρ is noted to be 0.9. Estimates are made in Table 3-2 using values of ρ of 0.8, 0.85, 0.9 and 0.95. Savings from the credit are of a much lower order of magnitude than savings from property tax exemption. An 11 percent tax credit (with $\rho = 0.9$) would be necessary to create a 5 percent savings to the firm, a typical savings with the property tax exemption.

Interest Subsidies

All interest subsidy programs enable the firm to finance some portion of a new facility at a lending rate below the conventional or market rate. If the entire facility can be financed in this manner, then the present value of the subsidized project cost can be expressed by equation (3.4), substituting the subsidy interest rate s for the conventional rate i. Savings to the firm from the subsidy can be calculated as the difference in present value costs of conventional and subsidy methods of financing, or

$$
S_{is}^* = \int_0^n \left\{ \left(\frac{i}{1 - e^{-in}} - \frac{s}{1 - e^{-sn}} \right) - T \left[\frac{i}{1 - e^{-in}} (1 - e^{-in}e^{it}) \right. \right.
$$

$$
\left. \left. - \frac{s}{1 - e^{-sn}} (1 - e^{-sn}e^{st}) \right] \right\} e^{-rt} \, dt , \tag{3.7}
$$

where $S_{is}^* =$ savings to the firm per dollar outlay resulting from the interest subsidy. Integrating equation (3.7) yields

$$
S_{is}^* = \frac{i(1 - e^{-rn})}{r(1 - e^{-in})} - \frac{s(1 - e^{-rn})}{r(1 - e^{-sn})} - T \left\{ \frac{i}{1 - e^{-in}} \left[\frac{1 - e^{-rn}}{r} \right. \right.
$$

$$
\left. - \frac{e^{-rn} - e^{-in}}{i - r} \right] - \frac{s}{1 - e^{-sn}} \left[\frac{1 - e^{-rn}}{r} - \frac{e^{-rn} - e^{-sn}}{s - r} \right] \right\}
$$

$$
\tag{3.7a}
$$

Although equation (3.7a) can be reduced further, the above expression highlights the nature of the interest subsidy. The first two terms on the right side of the equality sign express the reduction in loan repayments, and the third term (within braces) denotes the reduction in tax-deductible interest costs. The subsidy is the net impact of these two influences.

The reduced lending rate in an interest subsidy may be implicit when the facility is leased rather than owned by the tenant. Lease arrangements are common only in revenue bond financing, with a typical arrangement consisting of a public agency retaining title to the facility. In most states the choice between leasing and owning is stipulated by law and thus is not left up to the firm. This restricts the flexibility of revenue bond financing as a financial inducement.

A lease is of advantage to a firm that needs to conserve working capital or finds greater tax savings inherent in the lease agreement.[9] When the "own" option is elected in revenue bond financing or in loan and loan guarantee programs, a 100 percent financing plan is typically part of the program. Thus, conservation of working capital would not appear to be an important factor in determining relative advantages of leasing and owning to firms accepting an interest subsidy. Relative tax advantage, however, can be important and is analyzed by our model.

Consider again an investment K_o in a new facility to be financed by a lease arrangement. Let R = annual lease repayment. The lease will be amortized in a manner analogous to a loan [see equation (3.2)]:

$$K_o = \int_0^n Re^{-it}\, dt.$$ (3.8)

Integrating, we have

$$R = \frac{K_o i}{1 - e^{-in}}.$$ (3.8a)

Thus, the present value cost per dollar outlay, C_R^*, to a firm that leases its plant is

$$C_R^* = \int_0^n (1 - T)\left[A^*(t) + \frac{i}{1 - e^{-in}}\right]e^{-rt}\, dt.$$ (3.9)

The entire lease payment is tax deductible, but the tenant cannot depreciate the leased facility. Integrating equation (3.9) yields

$$C_R^* = (1 - T)\left[A^* + \frac{i(1 - e^{-rn})}{r(1 - e^{-in})}\right].$$ (3.9a)

Whether it is preferable to lease or own depends on the size of the principal amount of the lease versus the depreciation write-off because both are tax deductible when the relevant option is chosen. If the interest rate and project size are specified, principal is determined as well. The lease-versus-own decision then depends on the proportion of the facility that is depreciable. For any investment, there will be some percentage of depreciable property at which the prospective firm will be indifferent between leasing and owning. This percentage can be estimated, for different interest rates and

Table 3-3
Values of ρ That Equate Leasing and Owning

			$n = 20$		
			r		
i or s	0.06	0.08	0.10	0.12	0.14
0.02	0.77683	0.73425	0.70031	0.66684	0.64028
0.04	0.74836	0.69909	0.6572	0.62137	0.59087
0.06	0	0.66617	0.61923	0.57957	0.54528
0.08	*	0	0.58444	0.54076	0.50381
0.10	*	*	0	0.49497	0.46640

			$n = 30$		
			r		
i or s	0.06	0.08	0.10	0.12	0.14
0.02	0.70164	0.64706	0.60400	0.56989	0.54272
0.04	0.64538	0.58022	0.52919	0.48906	0.45735
0.06	0	0.52141	0.46401	0.40551	0.38430
0.08	*	0	0.40870	0.36066	0.32344
0.10	*	*	0	0.31233	0.27374

*Not economically relevant.

loan and lease maturities, by setting equations (3.4a) and (3.9a) equal to each other and solving for ρ. The result is

$$\rho = \frac{r^2 n^2 i}{2} \frac{(e^{-rn} - e^{-in})}{(r - i)(1 - e^{-in})(1 - rn - e^{-rn})} . \qquad (3.10)$$

The value of ρ that equates costs of leasing and owning is shown in Table 3-3 for various levels of borrowing rate and cost of capital and for financing of twenty and thirty years duration. It is assumed that the interest rate and replacement policy are the same whether leasing or owning.

From Appendix B, it is estimated that an average plant is composed of 90 percent depreciable property. Although there must be considerable variation about this figure, all the estimates in Table 3-3 are considerably below 90 percent. Since most plants are owned, whether financed by subsidy or not, the estimated figures appear logical. The reason that lease arrangements are common only in revenue bond financing is the attractiveness of the lease-with-property-tax-exemption format, and not because of a lease-versus-own type of decision discussed above. In analyzing individual subsidy programs, it will be assumed that the firm owns the interest subsidized facility, with the aforementioned exception.

Revenue Bond

Revenue bonds typically finance all project construction and acquisition costs. Thus, the savings a representative firm would reap from electing revenue bond financing are captured in equation (3.7a). The savings per dollar outlay can be estimated under various specified values of r, i, s, and n.

The relationship between i and s depends on supply and demand conditions in the corporate and municipal bond markets; probably the most important demand factor is the marginal income tax rates of bond buyers. Since 1950 the ratio of the municipal bond rate to the corporate bond rate has ranged from 0.64 to 0.80. In Table 3-4 s/i is fixed at 0.75, the average ratio for the period.

Bond maturity may vary considerably among issues. Of the thirty-nine states that reported their maximum permissible revenue bond maturities to the New York State Department of Commerce, six stated twenty-five years, fourteen stated thirty years, thirteen stated forty years, one stated fifty years, and six stated no limit. Because actual maturity may be considerably less than maximum,[d] n is set at twenty and thirty years in Table 3-4.

For twenty-year bonds, savings per dollar outlay range from 1.5 percent to 7.5 percent depending on subsidy and market interest rates and the firm's rate of discount. For thirty-year bonds, savings range from 1.6 percent to 9.5 percent. Compared to the tax subsidies analyzed earlier in this chapter, these savings are greater in magnitude than those from a 1 percent investment tax credit and in the range of a ten-year property tax exemption.

Revenue Bond-Property Tax Exemption Combination

As noted in Chapter 2, in many states revenue bond financing is provided for a prospective firm, but a nonprofit public corporation

---

[d] For example, although revenue bond maturity may be as great as fifty years in Massachusetts, the average maturity of bonds issued between 1967 and 1974 was 16.1 years.

Table 3-4
Savings to the Firm: Revenue Bond

				$n = 20$		
				r		
s	i	0.06	0.08	0.10	0.12	0.14
0.03	0.04	0.03147	0.02569	0.02129	0.01790	0.01525
0.04	0.053	0.04381	0.03594	0.02996	0.02534	0.02171
0.05	0.067	0.06067	0.05012	0.04198	0.03567	0.03071
0.06	0.08	Ind.[a]	Ind.[a]	0.05247	0.04475	0.03868
0.07	0.093	*	0.07543	0.06369	0.05441	0.04724

				$n = 30$		
				r		
s	i	0.06	0.08	0.10	0.12	0.14
0.03	0.04	0.03863	0.02988	0.02381	0.01945	0.01632
0.04	0.053	0.05512	0.04305	0.03464	0.02855	0.02420
0.05	0.067	0.07824	0.06161	0.04999	0.04148	0.03435
0.06	0.08	Ind.[a]	Ind.[a]	0.06362	0.05300	0.04554
0.07	0.093	*	0.09522	0.07810	0.06513	0.05635

[a]Indeterminate; a $0 \div 0$ form occurs in the calculations.
*Not economically relevant.

retains title to the project. The public corporation is exempt from property taxation, and the firm leases the facility from it. In some states the firm must make a payment in lieu of property taxes. In this case savings to the firm would be about the same as those generated when the firm owns the facility.[e] The case when a payment in lieu of taxes is not required is analyzed below.

In the lease-versus-own calculations made earlier, it was noted that the rational firm would usually prefer the "own" alternative. This is used as the conventional financing method; against it will be compared a lease with an implicit interest cost equivalent to that of a revenue bond. Savings generated include both an interest and tax subsidy. They are estimated by subtracting equation (3.9) (using the

[e]The interest subsidy in this case would be implicit in lower lease payments. Savings to the firm would be exactly the same as the revenue bond firm owns the facility case only if that firm were indifferent between leasing and owning.

subsidy interest rate s in place of i) from equation (3.4), adding equation (3.5) to the difference, and performing the integration. The result is

$$S^*_{rbpte} = \frac{(1 - T)(1 - e^{-rn})}{r} \left[\frac{i}{1 - e^{-in}} - \frac{s}{1 - e^{-sn}} + T_p\varepsilon \right]$$
$$- \frac{Ti(e^{-rn} - e^{-in})}{(r - i)(1 - e^{-in})} - \frac{2\rho T}{rn} \left[1 - \frac{1 - e^{-rn}}{rn} \right]. \quad (3.11)$$

Equation (3.11) contains seven parameters whose values have been set at different amounts in computing previous tables. To simplify matters, four parameters will be set at only one level: $n = 20$, $T_p = 0.02$, $\varepsilon = 1$ and $\rho = 0.9$. The others—i,s, and r—will be allowed to vary through the same range as in Table 3-5.

Note that the present value savings from the revenue bond and the tax exemption are additive. The portion of the original project composed of machinery and equipment has a typical average life of thirteen years. The portion composed of plant has a typical life of twenty-three years.[f] The average life of plant plus equipment, weighted by typical proportions of each, is about seventeen years, three years less than the depreciable life assumed for all capital in equation (3.11). The property tax exemption continues for the life of the facility, includes land, and is probably underestimated by setting $n = 20$. In calculating savings, these discrepancies will tend to offset each other.

Comparing Tables 3-4 and 3-5, it can be seen that at low rates of i, s, and r, the revenue bond-lease alternative is more attractive; at high rates the own alternative dominates. The principal cause of this phenomenon can be deduced by glancing at Table 3-3. As i, s, and r increase, the own option increasingly dominates the lease option. Were it not for the savings from the property tax exemption, the entries in the lower right portion of Table 3-5 would be negative. In this area the loss in depreciation deductibility from choosing the lease option outweighs the savings from the lower borrowing rate implicit in the lease option. For a specific combination of i, s, and r, savings to the firm will increase by decreasing ρ and increasing n, Tp, and ε (although ε is already set at its maximum value in Table 3-5).

---

[f]These estimates are derived from IRS guidelines. For their derivation, see Appendix B.

Table 3-5
Savings to the Firm: Revenue Bond (Lease)-Property Tax Exemption Combination
($n = 20$, $T_p = 0.02$, $\varepsilon = 1$, $\rho = 0.9$)

				r		
s	i	0.06	0.08	0.10	0.12	0.14
0.03	0.04	0.09731	0.06548	0.04247	0.02571	0.01347
0.04	0.053	0.10460	0.07018	0.04534	0.02728	0.01410
0.05	0.067	0.11676	0.07902	0.05182	0.03201	0.01751
0.06	0.08	0.12660	Ind.[a]	0.05696	0.03570	0.02016
0.07	0.093	*	0.09429	0.06308	0.04029	0.02366

[a]Indeterminate.
*Not economically relevant.

Low-Interest Loan: Bond Financed

Loan programs, as noted in Chapter 2, are financed either by tax-exempt bond issues or from state tax revenues. In the former, loans are made to firms at rates equal to or slightly above the state's borrowing rate. Loan programs differ from revenue bond programs in that only a fraction of project cost is financed by the low-interest loan. This fraction varies among and within states.

The modal value of this fraction is estimated by examining the two most widely used programs: those of Pennsylvania (tax financed) and New York (bond financed). In Pennsylvania, as in New York, the loan covers part of the acquisition cost of land and plant. From 1957 to 1969, Pennsylvania provided an average of 38 percent of land and plant costs at reduced lending rates. A local development agency was expected to contribute at least 10 percent, matching the state's lending rate. Thus approximately 50 percent of land and plant costs were financed by subsidy lending rates. When machinery and equipment cost are included among project costs for a typical plant, the proportion of total project costs financed at subsidy rates falls to roughly 25 percent.[g] The New York program follows similar guidelines.

[g]From Appendix B, the typical project consists of 53 percent machinery and equipment, in value terms. Inclusion of machinery and equipment in project costs lowers the portion financed by low-interest loans from 50 percent to about 25 percent.

To compute the savings to the firm that chooses loan financing, note that the cost of a conventional loan is expressed in equation (3.4). Further, the project cost to a firm accepting a low-interest loan can be approximated as the weighted sum of a conventional and a subsidized loan, the weights being the percentages of total cost financed by each method, or

$$
C_i^* = \int_0^n \left\{ (1 - T)A^*(t) + \frac{\lambda s}{1 - e^{-sn}} [1 - T(1 - e^{-sn}e^{st})] \right.
$$

$$
+ \frac{(1 - \lambda)i}{1 - e^{-in}} [1 - T(1 - e^{-in}e^{it})]
$$

$$
\left. - \rho T \left[\frac{2(n - t)}{n^2} \right] \right\} e^{-rt} dt,
\tag{3.12}
$$

where λ = percent of total costs financed by subsidized loan.
   Then, let

$$
a = \frac{i}{1 - e^{-in}} [1 - T(1 - e^{-in}e^{it})];
$$

$$
b = \frac{s}{1 - e^{-sn}} [1 - T(1 - e^{-sn}e^{st})].
$$

Subtracting equation (3.12) from equation (3.4) results in

$$
S_i^* = \int_0^n [a - \lambda b - (1 - \lambda)a]e^{-rt} dt
$$

$$
= \lambda \int_0^n (a - b)e^{-rt} dt
$$

$$
= \lambda \int_0^n \left\{ \left(\frac{i}{1 - e^{-in}} - \frac{s}{1 - e^{-sn}} \right) \right.
$$

$$
\left. - T \left[\frac{i}{1 - e^{-in}} (1 - e^{-in}e^{it}) - \frac{s}{1 - e^{-sn}} (1 - e^{-sn}e^{st}) \right] \right\} e^{-rt} dt,
$$

or equation (3.7) multiplied by λ. Integration yields (3.7a) multiplied by λ.
   Loan maturities vary from ten to twenty years. To compare savings from a bond-financed twenty-year loan with those from a twenty-year revenue bond, multiply the entries in Table 3-4 by 0.25. Savings from loans with fifteen-year maturities, perhaps more typi-

Table 3-6
Savings to the Firm: Loan Program Financed by Tax-Exempt Bonds
($n = 15, \lambda = 0.25$)

				r		
s	i	*0.06*	*0.08*	*0.10*	*0.12*	*0.14*
0.03	0.04	0.00606	0.00506	0.00437	0.00376	0.00326
0.04	0.053	0.00974	0.00831	0.00742	0.00543	0.00545
0.05	0.067	0.01251	0.01067	0.00921	0.00799	0.00701
0.06	0.08	Ind.[a]	Ind.[a]	0.01138	0.00988	0.00869
0.07	0.093	*	0.01571	0.01379	0.01189	0.01048

[a]Indeterminate
*Not economically relevant.

cal, are shown in Table 3-6. It is assumed that the spread between conventional and subsidy interest rates is the same as that in bond financing.

With one quarter of the project subsidized at reduced lending rates, and with the interest subsidy spread over a shorter time span, it is not surprising that this version of the loan program compares unfavorably to revenue bonds. Of more interest is the deeper interest subsidy in the tax-financed version.

Low-Interest Loan: Tax Financed

The prototype of this program is Pennsylvania's. Throughout most of its existence, loans were made at a 2 percent rate to recipient firms. Using the same parameters as in Table 3-6, savings to the firm at a 2 percent lending rate are shown in Table 3-7.

Savings under a 2 percent lending rate range up to 5 percent of the capital outlay, making this loan program nearly competitive with twenty-year revenue bonds. Increasing n or λ could enable a 2 percent rate loan program to generate equivalent or greater savings. Also, administrators of a tax-financed loan program do not feel constrained to limit a loan to $5 million per project, granting it greater flexibility than revenue bonds in this respect.

Table 3-7
Savings to the Firm: Loan Program Financed by Taxes
($n = 15$, $\lambda = 0.25$)

				r		
s	i	*0.06*	*0.08*	*0.10*	*0.12*	*0.14*
0.02	0.04	0.01304	0.01106	0.00946	0.00816	0.00709
0.02	0.05	0.02002	0.01699	0.01456	0.01257	0.01095
0.02	0.06	Ind.[a]	0.02318	0.01990	0.01720	0.01501
0.02	0.07	0.03433	0.02962	0.02547	0.02204	0.01925
0.02	0.08	0.04262	Ind.[a]	0.03128	0.02708	0.02369
0.02	0.09	0.05068	0.04322	0.03736	0.03232	0.02831

[a]Indeterminate.

Loan Guarantee

Loan guarantee programs, found primarily in New England, vary minimally among states in their operation. Most states reserve these funds for firms that cannot find financing elsewhere. The guarantee covers land, plant, and equipment. It typically finances up to 90 percent of the loan for plant and land and up to 80 percent of the loan for machinery and equipment. Maximum loan maturities are normally twenty-five years for the former and 10 years for the latter.

Because land and plant receive financing terms different from those for machinery and equipment, they must be separated when estimating savings to the firm. This can be done by specifying the cost of a guaranteed loan as

$$C_{lg}^* = \int_0^n \alpha[\lambda_1 b + (1 - \lambda_1)a] + (1 - \alpha)[\lambda_2 b + (1 - \lambda_2)a]$$

$$+ (1 - T)A^*(t) - \rho T\left[\frac{2(n - t)}{n^2}\right] e^{-rt} dt, \qquad (3.13)$$

where α = percent of project costs spent on land and plant; λ_1 = percent of loan for land and plant backed by the guarantee; λ_2 = percent of loan for machinery and equipment backed by the guarantee; a and b are defined above in equation (3.12).

Subtracting equation (3.13) from equation (3.4) and simplifying terms results in

$$S_{lg}^* = [\lambda_1\alpha + \lambda_2(1 - \alpha)]\int_0^n \left\{ \left(\frac{i}{1 - e^{-in}} - \frac{s}{1 - e^{-sn}} \right) \right.$$

$$\left. - T\left[\frac{i}{1 - e^{-in}}(1 - e^{-in}e^{it}) - \frac{s}{1 - e^{-sn}}(1 - e^{-sn}e^{st}) \right] \right\} e^{-rt}\,dt\,,$$

or equation (3.7) multiplied by the set of coefficients within brackets. Integrating yields equation (3.7a) multiplied by the coefficient set. Different loan maturities may be approximated by specifying different values of n and carrying out the integration separately for land and plant versus machinery and equipment.

Although there will in reality be only one loan and one interest rate encompassing the guaranteed and nonguaranteed portions of the project, it is asserted that the rate will depend on the percentage of the loan that the state guarantees. The premium paid by the firm for the state guarantee is implicit in s, the subsidy lending rate.

Specifying the subsidy and conventional interest rates is problematic. In the real world of a less than perfectly elastic supply of loanable funds, not all firms that wish to borrow will obtain funds at an appropriate interest rate. Because loan guarantee programs are usually tailored for firms that cannot obtain a conventional loan, estimating savings to such a firm becomes an impossible task. Even if the firm could obtain a conventional loan at a higher interest rate, neither the conventional or subsidy rate nor their relationship to each other can be prespecified as accurately as they were in the revenue bond and loan progams. Thus the estimates of savings to the firm in Table 3-8 must be examined in this light. In this table borrowing rates are limited to higher levels to reflect the riskiness of the borrower, and the guaranteed rate is set three percentage points lower than the conventional rate. ρ, λ_1, and λ_2 are set at 0.5, 0.9, and 0.8, respectively.

For the ranges of i in Table 3-8, loan guarantees can be ranked favorably with revenue bonds and slightly above low-interest loans. If the spread between i and s were less, this would no longer be true.

Table 3-8
Savings to the Firm: Loan Guarantee Program
($n = 20$ [land and plant], $n = 10$ [machinery and equipment], $\alpha = 0.5$,
$\lambda_1 = 0.9$, $\lambda_2 = 0.8$)

				r		
s	i	*0.06*	*0.08*	*0.10*	*0.12*	*0.14*
0.06	0.09	Ind.[a]	0.06758	0.05826	0.05079	0.04474
0.07	0.10	*	0.07000	Ind.[a]	0.05280	0.04661
0.08	0.11	*	Ind.[a]	0.06256	0.05472	0.04839
0.09	0.12	*	*	0.06403	Ind.[a]	0.05008
0.10	0.13	*	*	Ind.[a]	0.05830	0.05177

[a]Indeterminate.
*Not economically relevant.

The Federal Investment Tax Credit

The federal investment tax credit, like depreciation of long-lived assets, reduces tax liability for the owner of the assets. Thus it is not available to the firm that leases its facility from a public entity and should be deducted from the savings of such a firm when it accepts a subsidy. If the firm owns the facility, the tax credit is available whether it accepts a subsidy or not, and does not affect the results.

Since 1962 an investment tax credit has been legislated into and out of existence several times. It has been in effect at different percentage rates and under different qualifying criteria. Although it is impossible to characterize a typical form of tax credit among all these changes, one point is clear; the existence of a federal investment tax credit substantially reduces the advantages of revenue bond-lease financing.

Currently there exists a 10 percent credit on new investment other than buildings. The value of the credit is reduced if the useful life of the qualifying property is less than seven years. A firm constructing a new facility would be able to utilize the credit on property representing about half the value of the facility, creating a tax savings of up to 5 percent of the cost of the project. Similarly, under the former 7 percent credit, savings of up to 3.5 percent would occur. When in effect, the investment tax credit reduces savings from the revenue bond-property tax exemption subsidy to the point where it is normally no more desirable than a loan guarantee or a Pennsylvania-style loan program.

Costs of the Incentives

Besides knowing the relative strengths of various inducements at its disposal, the state or local government must know their relative costs if it is to obtain the highest return from its subsidy dollar. In terms of costs to the government body extending the subsidy, incentive programs vary considerably.

Revenue bonds cost the state nothing other than the administrative expenses of the program. The subsidy to a firm that accepts revenue bond financing is borne by the federal government as foregone tax revenue from the bondholders. The bondholders do not bear any real cost because the bond purchase represents a voluntary transfer. Naturally, heavy use of revenue bonds can force up municipal borrowing rates. It has been argued that this phenomenon occurred in the mid-1960s before restrictions were placed on revenue bond financing.

Loan programs financed by general obligation bonding are also relatively costless to the state. If one assumes that the state's opportunity cost of funds is its borrowing rate, then there is no subsidy cost in granting loans at or slightly above that rate. However, there are costs of defaults[h] and, if the program is used heavily, a possible reduction in the state's bond rating. Administrative costs are likely to be similar to those of a revenue bond program.

A state employing loan guarantees creates an insurance fund (usually by issuing bonds) to provide for coverage of possible defaults. Because an insurance premium is attached by the state to the guaranteed loan rate, the program can be self-financing. If defaults exceed premium income, the insurance funds must be drawn upon. The state bears the majority of the costs of default, but the federal government loses tax revenue if the tax-exempt bonds are required to bail out defaults in the private sector. Administrative costs should be comparable to loan and revenue bond programs.

A Pennsylvania-style loan program is more costly to the state. In

---

[h] In many cases the state is able to obtain another tenant for the facility and thus avoid default costs.

addition to administrative and default costs, the state incurs a substantial loss every time it makes a loan at less than its opportunity cost of funds. The administrative costs of Pennsylvania's loan program averaged $131,500 in the first nine years of its existence.[10] This is roughly equal to the interest foregone by the state in one year on one $3.5-million loan, assuming a 2 percent lending rate and a 6 percent cost of funds. Thus, the Pennsylvania program is considerably less efficient, per dollar lent, than other programs discussed above.

All interest subsidies reduce a firm's interest deductions from federal and state income tax liability, and they thus increase tax revenues when firms accept these subsidies. To the extent that municipal bond financing is used to generate the funds lent by the state, these tax gains may be offset by the greater tax losses incurred when investors purchase these bonds as tax shelters.

Most inefficient of all programs are tax subsidies. Each dollar of subsidy to the firm is also a dollar of revenue lost to state or local government. For a property tax exemption, it is typically the municipality that incurs the revenue loss. For an investment tax credit, it is the state. To these, administrative costs must be added.

Because property taxes are normally deductible from federal and state income tax liability, a firm accepting an exemption will pay more income taxes to both levels of government. A firm accepting a state investment tax credit will reduce its state income tax liability but increase its federal liability because it has less state tax to deduct.

Unlike revenue bonds and certain other interest subsidies, the cost of tax subsidies is borne by the government offering them. As a corollary, both the federal government and the recipient firm benefit when a state or local government grants a tax subsidy. Thus, the argument that state inducements to industry represent a raid on federal coffers is somewhat specious. It depends on the nature of the subsidy.

Effects of Financial Incentives on Location

The reader has already been warned to place less faith in the numerical estimates of savings per dollar outlay for any inducement than in the ordinal rankings of inducements predicted by the estimates.

Nevertheless, savings per dollar outlay can be considered as the maximum locational project cost disadvantage that can be overcome by the inducement. For example, if other costs do not differ between locations, financing with a thirty-year revenue bond (with $r = 0.08$ and $s = 0.07$) can induce a firm to relocate to an otherwise more costly site if the cost differential is less than 9.5 percent between the two locations (Table 3-4).

Stober and Falk made a further refinement of this approach. For each of the two-digit manufacturing Standard Industrial Classifications, they estimated the amount of labor cost differential that can be equalized by any incentive by multiplying the average ratio of capital to labor costs for each industry by the savings per dollar outlay created by the incentive.[11] Their estimates of ratios of capital to labor costs can be applied to estimates of savings from incentive programs made in this chapter. For very labor-intensive industries, the labor cost differential that can be overcome by incentives ranges up to 1.6 percent. For very capital-intensive industries, labor cost differentials from 1 percent to 19 percent can be equalized, depending on the strength of the incentive.

Based on applications of the model developed in this chapter, one can by no means reject the hypothesis that incentives cannot influence location or investment decisions. Verification, however, requires careful empirical testing. Several empirical tests will be made in Chapter 4.

Summary

In this chapter a model was developed that was used to estimate savings to a representative or typical firm per dollar outlay on a new facility if it accepts a financial incentive instead of, or in conjunction with, conventional financing. These estimates depend on specification of parameters in the model and are subject to variation; however, it does appear that the more effective types of incentives can possibly influence location and investment decisions.

It was shown that revenue bond and property tax exemption incentives (and a combination of the two) provided the greatest savings per dollar outlay on land, plant, and equipment. A federal investment tax credit substantially reduces the effectiveness of the revenue bond-property tax exemption combination. A Pennsylvania-type loan program was less effective. Loan programs in which funds were lent at tax-exempt interest rates and a state investment tax credit provided minimal financial benefits to a firm accepting them. Less confidence was placed in estimates of savings per dollar outlay from a guaranteed loan because of the difficulty in specifying the spread between conventional and subsidy interest rates. The estimates in this chapter place them just below revenue bonds and property tax exemptions in effectiveness. This ranking of programs reflects existing guidelines and methods of implementation. For example, a loan program, if it financed the entire facility at a 2 percent lending rate, would become more effective than other programs.

The above ranking in terms of effectiveness of programs must be tempered by a consideration of their relative costs. Only revenue bonds provide a strong financial incentive to firms and are virtually costless to the government body issuing them. A loan guarantee program incurs minimal costs and was ranked as relatively effective. Two other subsidies shown to be effective—property tax exemptions and Pennsylvania-type loans—are costly to offer, especially tax exemptions.

A bond-financed loan program and an investment tax credit provided little financial incentive. In addition, the former is relatively costless, the latter quite costly per dollar of subsidy.

4 Macroeconomic Estimates of Program Effectiveness

In this chapter we attempt to estimate the impact of various incentive programs on aggregate state investment. The focus is macroeconomic in the sense that we are not concerned here with the composition of the investment spending by industry or with the distribution of spending by geographic areas within the state. The question examined is simply, Do inducement programs affect total investment in the state offering the incentive? A related question, which we also examine, is whether inducement programs affect investment in neighboring states that do not offer incentives. In addition, cost-benefit analysis of the various programs to the granting state is performed. Three prototype programs are analyzed: a loan guarantee program, direct loans, and industrial development bonds. Property tax exemptions are not examined because of difficulties in obtaining requisite data and because they have been shown to be an inefficient form of subsidy—that is, the cost savings to the recipient firm is less than the direct outlay of the grantor. The investment tax credit is not analyzed because of its inefficiency and infrequent use. It would be rational, then, for states or communities to opt for alternative programs. These we examine.

Measuring Induced Investment: The Models

In order to evaluate the effectiveness of the incentive programs in attracting investment, we must specify what investment would have been in the absence of the program. Several alternative ways of answering the questions, each with its particular strengths and weaknesses, are discussed below.

Questionnaires

One approach to the problem is to ask those firms participating in the program what their investment would have been if they had not received the benefit of the inducement. This has been the method employed in the few major studies that have attempted to measure the amount of investment induced.[1] A problem in the questionnaire approach is that businessmen tend to overstate the importance of incentive programs because they hope their support will encourage states and local governments to expand their programs. The problem is not unlike that of attempting to ascertain the role of state and local taxes in location decision; those factors amendable by public action receive a disproportionate amount of verbal attack or praise. There is the additional problem of constructing questions that elicit sufficient and accurate responses.[2]

Comparative Cost Studies

While not implemented to our knowledge, an alternative approach would be to compute the cost savings resulting from the incentive to those firms that participated in the program and compare this figure against the cost differential incurred in moving away from the least-cost site in order to take advantage of the program. This would indicate where and by how much the program made a difference and facilitated investment. In effect, this approach gives the same information as the questionnaire but supports the answers with facts and figures. The obvious problem is the practical difficulty of implementing a comparative cost study. It involves identifying, for each participating firm, the least cost location and calculating cost differences between that and the actual location.[3] For one firm alone such a study is a formidable task. This kind of approach has been used in the past to calculate hypothetical cost savings to firms, but the crucial stage of linking cost savings to location cost differentials has not been reached.[4]

Explicit Investment Function

Each of the above techniques involves working on a firm-by-firm basis, which is both tedious and limited because of the problems involved in generalizing from the firm to the industry. This suggests that while it is difficult to specify the amount that any one firm would invest in a state, it may be possible to specify the amount that all firms together would invest in the region—that is, it may be possible to define, for a state, an investment function that would relate aggregate industry investment in the state to various variables which presumably affect incentives to invest. Inducement programs could be then entered as explanatory variables in the equation and their significance examined statistically. An investment function could be specified for total investment or, with more difficulty, for investment by industry.

A major difficulty is specifying a regional investment function, at any level of aggregation. Specification and estimation of investment functions for countries have received a good deal of attention in the econometric literature.[5] Comparable work on a subnational level does not exist because investment incentives or opportunities in any one region must be compared against alternatives in other regions. In spite of these difficulties we attempt to estimate, for each of the states under study, an aggregate state investment function for manufacturing industries:

$$I_t = f(x_1, x_2, \ldots, x_n) \tag{4.1}$$

where I_t = total investment by manufacturing industries in year t, and $x_1, x_2, \ldots, x_n$ = factors that affect state investment, including the inducement program.

The explicit investment function approach fits a traditional investment function to state data while attempting to account for the effect of the inducement program. The most commonly used model of investment has been the accelerator theory.[6] It states that the change in a firm's capital stock between two points in time (or net investment during that period) is proportional to the difference between desired and actual capital stock at the same point in time. The version used below states that the adjustment of desired actual capital stock does not occur immediately. Rather, net investment is determined by differences between desired and actual capital stock over several past periods—that is, investment is a distributed lag function of past differences in desired and actual capital stock. Because desired capital stock cannot be measured, it is assumed that the difference between desired and actual capital stock is proportional to the change in value added between the same two points in time. Thus the basic accelerator model hypothesizes that investment is a function of lagged changes in value added. The effect of the inducement program is described by either the amount lent or the total project cost of all subsidized investments. The inducement variable is also entered in lagged form, implying a time interval between the granting of the inducement and the investment spending.

Different measures of desired capital stock and other determinants of investment behavior have been used in investment models. When estimating state investment functions, choice of independent variable is somewhat limited because several (capacity utilization, index of industrial production, and capital stock, for example) are not routinely published for individual states. Other variables, such as the interest rate, are not subject to substantial variation regionally, and national data represent adequate proxies. For states, the investment time series data are reported annually (not quarterly like the U.S. time series), making it more difficult to specify the lag structure and creating degrees of freedom problems.

The advantage of the explicit function is that it provides a theoretically justifiable predictor of the investment time series. If a lagged inducement variable is entered into the accelerator model and has no significant effect on investment, one cannot accept the hypothesis that inducement programs affect the level of investment. If the lagged inducement variable is significant with a positive coefficient, one cannot reject the hypothesis that the inducement program has created new investment, without further evidence. Since the accelerator theory should predict changes in the level of investment under existing economic conditions, entry of lagged inducement variables with no significant effect on investment implies that the investment financed by the inducement program represented only projects that would have occurred in the absence of the inducement program. Similarly, a positive significant coefficient implies that the program created new investment.

Such a conclusion is valid only when there is no problem about the direction of causality—that is, when the growth of the inducement program is not directly linked to the economic growth of the state. Reverse causality could cause positive significant coefficients to occur for spurious reasons. In this case, one could not predict the effect of the program from the equation coefficients. A way of testing for this bias and a further check on the time series results is to use a dummy variable in place of aggregate loans and project costs. The dummy variable approach is explained below.

Implicit Investment Function

As a check on the evidence provided by the explicit state investment functions, it is possible to construct implicit functions. Again, inducement programs can be entered into the investment functions as explanatory variables, their importance assessed, and results compared. Two alternative proxy-type functions are available:

1. Relate investment in the state to investment in the nation. This involves the assumption that investment will grow in the state at the same rate that it grows in the nation; those unspecified forces that operate on investment in the nation as a whole will operate similarly on a part of the whole, creating the same investment pattern. This assumption is more likely to hold true for total investment than for investment in any particular industry and in states that are most nearly microcosms of the national economy.

2. Relate investment in the state to time. Here the emphasis is on the peculiarity of the region and the regulatory of the investment pattern through time, while the other approach focuses on the similarity of the region to the national experience and permits any temporal pattern. The advantage is that it breaks the tie between the state and the nation, recognizing possibilities for real differences in investment experience, but forces the assumption that time is an adequate proxy for all those variables that affect investment. While it may capture some, such as the effect of capital stock on replacement investment, it may not sufficiently represent others. In addition, while it permits states to be relatively attractive or unattractive investment sites vis-à-vis other states, it does not permit comparative advantages to alter through time.

Equations (4.2) through (4.5) below describe the implicit investment functions. Each utilizes the dummy variable approach to measure program effectiveness rather than program size. A problem may exist in using program size as an explanatory variable when very few constraints are placed upon qualifying firms. In such cases it is reasonable to assume that program size, measured, for example, by the dollar value of lending, and dollars invested are going to be strongly correlated whether the program is effective or not. To take an extreme case, if all firms receive complete loans, program size and investment are perfectly correlated and the coefficient of the size variable would be equal to one. But it is incorrect to conclude that each dollar of loan caused one dollar of investment. Each dollar of investment is associated with one dollar of loan, but no causality is indicated. The effectiveness of the program cannot be unraveled from the necessary association between the two magnitudes. Lagging program size may alleviate the problem but not remove it. In such cases it is preferable to use the dummy variable technique:

$$I_t^j = \alpha + \beta t + \gamma D_t \qquad (4.2)$$

$$I_t^j = \alpha + \beta t + \delta Z_t \qquad (4.3)$$

where I_t^j = total manufacturing investment in state j in year t

D_t = dummy variable

= 0 if no program in year t

= 1 if program in operation in year t

$Z_t = D_t t$

γ in equation (4.2) measures the shift in the state investment function with the introduction of an inducement program. δ in equation (4.3) measures the change in the rate at which state investment grows through time.

The other implicit investment function can be similarly used to evaluate program effectiveness:

$$I_t^j = \alpha + \beta(I_t^{us} - I_t^j) + \gamma D_t \qquad (4.4)$$

$$I_t^j = \alpha + \beta(I_t^{us} - I_t^j) + \delta Z_t \qquad (4.5)$$

where $(I_t^{us} - I_t^j)$ = national manufacturing investment in year t, net of manufacturing investment in state j, year t,[a]

$Z_t = D_t(I_t^{us} - I_t^j)$.

Induced Investment by Industry

A third technique used is to measure induced investment by industry. Adequate specification of an explicit state investment function

---

[a] Netting of state investment from the right side of the equation is necessary for purposes of regression analysis. The minimum requirement to assure consistency of the classical least squares estimator is that the disturbance term and the regressors are contemporaneously uncorrelated, a requirement that is violated when the same variable appears on both sides of the equation.

by industry was considered to be beyond the scope and capabilities of the study. Implicit functions linking state investment in each industry to time or to national investment in the industry seemed inadequate. Therefore a combination of an implicit investment function based on a fixed relationship with another region, not necessarily the nation, and a fixed relationship within the region through time was developed to estimate the amount of state investment that would be expected in the absence of an inducement program. Induced investment by industry can then be calculated as the difference between the actual investment and the amount expected.

The technique involves identification of one or more states comparable in growth performance to the state under study before that state introduced an inducement program. Assuming that the similarity in growth patterns would continue through time, except for the influence of inducement, expected investment in the absence of the program can be estimated based on investment in the comparable region. Any difference between the amount of investment that actually took place in the industrial inducement state and that which was predicted based on comparable states' performances could be attributed to introduction of the program. The technique involves five steps, done on an industry-by-industry basis:

1. Identification of the "reference region" based on comparisons of growth in employment, value added, and investment.
2. Determination of the relationship between investment in the reference region and investment in the study state prior to the introduction of an inducement program, using the ratio of average annual investment growth.
3. Calculation of investment growth in the reference region during the period after inducements are introduced in the study state.
4. Estimation of expected investment in the state in the absence of the program based on steps 3 and 2.
5. Estimation of induced investment as the difference between actual investment and the result of step 4.

Measuring Induced Investment: The Results

In this section we present the results of the application of the various investment models to examine the effectiveness of three programs.

One representative example of each program was investigated. We selected each state because the program we wished to study there was well established and was the only or dominant incentive. Our criteria for program analysis led us to select for study Connecticut (loan guarantee), Pennsylvania (loan), and Kentucky (revenue bond). In Connecticut, lending activity began in 1963, and investment data for 1954-1972 were used. In Pennsylvania, lending activity began in 1957. Although investment data were available for 1951-1972, we examined only the 1951-1969 period because a second important incentive program was introduced after 1969. In Kentucky, lending activity began in 1950; investment data were available and used for 1951-1972. Because of the longevity of Kentucky's program it was impossible to collect investment data for a preprogram reference region; an estimate of induced investment by industry could not be made.

The Connecticut Loan Guarantee Program

Explicit Investment Function. The explicit investment function described was estimated for Connecticut for the period 1954-1972, using deflated investment, value added, interest rate, and loan guarantee data.[7] State investment was regressed against lagged values of changes in value added and lagged values of loans guaranteed.

Before the Connecticut program (and those of the other states) was analyzed, the accelerator model was tested for applicability to state data. One of the problems in the examination of regional investment behavior is the difficulty of specifying a function that appropriately identifies incentives to invest in the region. As a check on the adequacy, the basic accelerator model was estimated for each of the states and for the nation. The results indicated that the model provided a reasonably accurate explanation of state investment patterns. In fact, the model explained more of the variance of the investment variable for the three study states than it did for national investment over the same time period.[b] We thus felt it appropriate to use this type of function to evaluate program effectiveness in the various states.

The explicit investment equations estimated for Connecticut

---

[b] For the United States, the best fitting equation possessed an $\bar{R}^2$ of 0.24. Compare to the $\bar{R}^2$s for the first equations in Tables 4-1, 4-4, and 4-7.

indicated that the loan guarantee program had no net effect on state investment. The coefficients of lagged loan variables were statistically insignificant when entered in a variety of equation forms. The loan variable for Connecticut had a value of zero for the period 1954-1963, when no loan guarantee program existed, and was equal to the value of loans guaranteed for each of the years 1963-1972. Equations (4.6) and (4.7) are examples of the explicit investment functions that were estimated, before and after including program variables.

$$I_t = \alpha_0 + \sum_{i=0}^{3} \alpha_i \Delta VA_{t-i} + \sum_{j=0}^{2} \alpha_j i_{t-j} \qquad (4.6)$$

$$I_t = \alpha_0 + \sum_{i=0}^{3} \alpha_i \Delta VA_{t-i} + \sum_{j=0}^{2} \alpha_j i_{t-j} + \sum_{k=0}^{2} \alpha_k L_{t-k} \qquad (4.7)$$

where I_t = total investment spending in manufacturing industries in year t; ΔVA_{t-i} = change in value added between year $t - i$ and $t - i - 1$; i_{t-j} = rate of interest in year $t - j$; L_{t-k} = dollar amount of loans guaranteed in year $t - k$.

The regression results are shown in Table 4-1. Although it possesses the wrong sign according to theory, the interest rate lagged one year was included in the model because it improved the equation fit and the structure of the lagged value-added coefficients. In a number of regressions of equation (4.7), lagged values of guaranteed loans were entered, but they were always statistically insignificant.[c] Two examples of equation (4.7) are shown. Even when entered alone, guaranteed loans showed no impact on investment spending. These results strongly suggest that the loan guarantee program did not induce investment in Connecticut.

Implicit Investment Function. Similar evidence is provided by the use of the implicit investment function model. Equations (4.2) to (4.5) were estimated by ordinary least squares for Connecticut using observations on investment activity from 1954 to 1972. The loan guarantee program was in operation for the last ten years of the observation period, 1963-1972. The estimates are presented in Table 4-2. The loan program had no separate effect on either the intercept

[c] A t value less than approximately 1.7-1.8 (varies slightly given the number of parameters estimated and the number of years' data used in the regressions) indicates the estimated parameter is not statistically significant at the 5 percent level for a one-tail probability.

Table 4-1
Estimates of Explicit Investment Functions for Connecticut
(Coefficient and t-Statistic)

Equation Form	Intercept	ΔVA_t	ΔVA_{t-1}	ΔVA_{t-2}	ΔVA_{t-3}	i_{t-1}	L_t	L_{t-1}	L_{t-2}	$\bar{R}^2$	n
4.6	−5.550 (−0.127)	0.076[a] (2.673)	0.117[a] (4.353)	0.079[a] (2.794)	0.076[b] (2.310)	40.753[a] (5.262)				0.66	19
4.7	53.117 (0.787)	0.039 (0.893)	0.086[b] (2.326)	0.046 (1.172)	0.056 (1.552)	29.150[b] (2.141)	−0.836 (−0.162)	0.345 (0.062)	11.051 (1.614)	0.66	19
4.7	−14.464 (−0.255)	0.082[b] (2.161)	0.121[a] (3.775)	0.083[b] (2.420)	0.074[b] (2.017)	43.105[a] (3.830)	−2.074 (−0.379)	−0.177 (−0.030)		0.61	19

[a]Significant at 1% level or greater.
[b]Significant at 5% level.

Table 4-2
Estimates of Implicit Investment Functions for Connecticut
(Coefficient and t-Statistic)

Equation Form	Intercept	t	D_t	$D_t t$	$I_t^{us} - I_t^j$	$(I_t^{us} - I_t^j)D_t$	$\bar{R}^2$	n
4.2	182.083[a] (6.188)	2.162 (0.469)	72.349 (1.432)				0.39	19
4.3	196.826[a] (5.352)	−0.403 (−0.600)		6.419 (1.324)			0.38	19
4.4	−6.887 (−0.164)			−30.087 (−1.019)	0.020[a] (4.952)		0.76	19
4.5	−31.936 (−0.543)				0.023[a] (3.799)	−0.003 (−1.085)	0.76	19

[a]Significant at 1% level or better.

or the slope of the function describing the relationship between investment and time; the coefficients of the dummy variables ($\hat{\gamma}$ and $\hat{\delta}$) are not significantly different from zero at 5 percent. The investment function relating Connecticut activity to adjusted national investment spending performs better than a time trend for Connecticut as measured by the $\bar{R}^2$s. However, the dummy variable coefficients again are not significantly different from zero. All of the evidence provided by the implicit investment functions thus indicates that the Connecticut loan guarantee program has had no significant effect on aggregate investment in the state.

Induced Investment by Industry. Because the overall Connecticut program is small, when dealing with induced investment by industry we had to limit the investigation to those industries in which program activity was large enough to expect a perceptible impact. For this purpose only industries in which there had been five or more guaranteed loans were considered, unless the number of commitments represented more than 1 percent of the number of establishments in the industry. Given this constraint, induced investment by industry over the period 1963-1967 and during 1969 was estimated using the methodology described above; the magnitudes are presented in Table 4-3.[d] The total amount of induced investment is estimated to be only $136,000 measured in real terms. A number of this mag-

[d] The year 1968 had to be omitted from the analysis because no state investment figures by industry were available for that year.

Table 4-3
Induced Investment by Industry in Connecticut, 1963-1967 and 1969

SIC Code*	Industry Name	Real Value of Induced Investment (thousands of dollars)
20	Food and kindred products	12,034
22	Textile mill products	−3,509
30	Rubber and miscellaneous plastic products	10,328
32	Stone, clay, glass, and concrete products	6,131
34	Fabricated metal products, except ordnance, machinery, and transportation equipment	43,769
35	Machinery, except electrical	36,484
36	Electrical machinery, equipment, and supplies	−30,514
37	Transportation equipment	17,788
38	Professional, scientific, and controlling instruments; photographic and optical goods; watches and clocks	−92,375
		+136

*Standard Industrial Classification Code

nitude is virtually insignificant in a program that over the same period committed more than $30 million on projects costing more than $40 million.

Thus, the evidence provided by each of the three approaches taken consistently indicates that the Connecticut loan guarantee program is ineffective in increasing total manufacturing investment in the state. As we suggest in Table 4-3, the program appears to substitute investment in some industries for that in others with a net effect of approximately zero.

The Pennsylvania Loan Program

Explicit Investment Function. Investment behavior in Pennsylvania in each year from 1951 through 1969 was estimated as a function of lagged values of changes in value added and lagged values of money

Table 4-4
Estimates of Explicit Investment Functions for Pennsylvania
(Coefficient and t-Statistic)

Equation Form	Intercept	ΔVA_t	ΔVA_{t-1}	ΔVA_{t-2}	ΔVA_{t-3}	L_t	L_{t-1}	$\bar{R}^2$	n
4.6	784.723[a]	0.051	0.175[a]	0.154[a]	0.139[a]			0.60	19
	(12.014)	(1.039)	(3.674)	(3.318)	(2.956)				
4.7	781.134[a]	0.014	0.122[b]	0.108[b]	0.087[b]	10.909[b]		0.70	19
	(13.842)	(0.287)	(2.616)	(2.476)	(2.001)	(2.398)			
4.7	782.058[a]	0.030	0.126[a]	0.101[b]	0.091[b]		11.763[b]	0.71	19
	(14.210)	(0.704)	(2.847)	(2.298)	(2.080)		(2.594)		

[a]Significant at 1% level or better.
[b]Significant at 5% level.

lent in the program. A good fit for the accelerator model was obtained without the use of an interest rate variable, which again possessed a positive coefficient. For the state the results of the explicit investment function approach were quite different from those of Connecticut. The loan program variable was always significant and positive when the amount lent in a single year was included in the accelerator model. However, due to problems of multicollinearity, when more than one year of the lagged loan variable was entered in the equation, all became statistically insignificant. In investigating the explicit investment function, lags in the loan variable from the current time period to three time periods were tried. Best results were achieved with current period loans and a one-year lag. The estimates of the parameters of the two best equations are presented in Table 4-4. The variables are defined analogously to equations (4.6) and (4.7) of Connecticut's explicit investment function.

The multicollinearity problem implies that although investment in any time period should be affected by loan activity over several recent years, we are constrained to look only at the coefficient of the loan variable for any one year. This coefficient is reasonably uniform in size, suggesting that effects of loans in years excluded from the equation tend to be reflected in the coefficient of the included loan variable. The coefficients of the loan variable in the equation may come close to picking up the entire effect of the program.

At first glance, the magnitude of the loan coefficients appears unrealistically large. For instance, equation 4.7 implies that, for every dollar lent in the Pennsylvania loan program, about eleven dollars of new investment that would otherwise not have occurred was induced. The size of the coefficient is due, at least in part, to the nature of the Pennsylvania program. If the loan program financed the entire investment, the coefficient should not be greater than one unless there is a substantial "multiplier" effect—that is, the loan-financed investment causes investment in related industries by creating new demand for intermediate or raw materials or for new services. In Pennsylvania, state loans finance only a proportion of expenditures on land and plant. Thus, the remainder of land and plant expenditures and all of equipment expenditures on the loan-financed project would be included in the multiplier effect. The average proportion of loan to total land and plant costs in Pennsylvania from 1957 to 1969 was 38 percent. The average proportion of land and plant expenditures to total expenditures has been estimated at 47 percent (Appendix B). From these figures one can deduce that if all loans caused new investment, the multiplier effect within the loan-financed projects only would predict a coefficient of six in the regression equations.[e]

This coefficient is more than half of the actual regression coefficients, and indirect multiplier effects have not yet been considered. This project multiplier effect is borne out by the results of some additional regression equations tested. In place of loans, total costs of the investment in plant were employed as an independent variable. For equation (4.7) above, the loan coefficient of 11.76 corresponded to a plant cost coefficient of 4.52, when all other variables in the equation remained unaltered. The ratio of total plant costs to loans over the 1959-1969 period was 100/38, or 2.63. One would expect the ratio of regression coefficients to reflect this relationship as more of the project cost is embedded in the equation and the coefficient drops. In fact, the ratio of the loan to plant cost coefficient is 2.60, extremely accurate in view of the statistical nature of the regression equation.

Of course, not all loans will necessarily create investment that would not have otherwise occurred. Sazama, in his questionnaire study, estimated that 43 percent of the state loans were "crucial," that is, they created investment that would not otherwise have

---

[e]Every dollar lent causes, on the average, spending on plant in the ratio of 100/38 and additional spending on equipment in the ratio of 100/47. Thus the project "multiplier" on a dollar lent is $1 \times 100/38 \times 100/47 = 5.60$.

occurred.[f] A loan coefficient of 11 would imply, assuming Sazama's figure is correct, an indirect multiplier of 4.6, a figure probably outside the realm of possibility. With a program that finances at reduced interest rates only 25 percent of total project costs, one might expect that the proportion of induced investment would be low, perhaps considerably lower than Sazama's estimate. If this is true, the loan and project cost coefficients will indeed be overstated. Several reasons might create this result.

First, to the extent that some of the forces affecting investment not explained by changes in value added are picked up by the loan coefficient, this coefficient might be biased above the true program effect. Another possibility is that the loan coefficient might be reflecting the mathematical relationship between loans and investment rather than a possible causal relationship running from loans to investment. If such a "casual" relationship exists, the regression coefficient will be biased upward. With the Connecticut program, which is much smaller and more restricted in scope, this was not a problem. As a further check on the results, a dummy variable was inserted in the accelerator model in place of the loan variable in order to avoid the causal versus casual relationship problem. It was inserted both separately and in a multiplicative relationship with the change in value-added variable. The dummy variable was assigned a value of zero for 1951-1956 (no program) and a value of one for 1956-1969 (program in effect). In all equations tested except one, the dummy variable coefficient was statistically insignificant. This result obviously weakens the validity of the time series approach. However, a variable constrained to equal one cannot possess as much explanatory power as a variable equal to the actual amount lent every year. In addition, the dummy variable coefficients were positive and generally approached levels of significance. The net result of application of the explicit investment function is thus rather ambiguous; while there is some indication of a positive impact from the program, those results are not without qualification.

Implicit Investment Function. The implicit investment function approach yields somewhat similar evidence. Results of estimation of equations (4.2) through (4.5) are presented in Table 4-5. Observa-

---

[f]Note that 43 percent of all loans does not necessarily imply 43 percent of all loan-financed investment. To the extent that crucial loans differ from noncrucial loans in average size, the 43 percent figure cannot be applied to investment figures without error.

Table 4-5

Estimates of Implicit Investment Functions for Pennsylvania

(Coefficient and t-Statistic)

Equation Form	Intercept	t	D_t	$D_t t$	$I_t^{us} - I_t^j$	$(I_t^{us} - I_t^j)D_t$	$\bar{R}^2$	n
4.2	831.576ᵃ (9.030)	52.690ᵃ (3.598)	−360.632ᵇ (−2.090)				0.42	19
4.3	783.592ᵃ (5.889)	40.964 (0.853)		−11.356 (−0.276)			0.26	19
4.4	237.130ᵇ (2.451)		−105.178 (−1.637)		0.068ᵃ (8.636)		0.81	19
4.5	151.850 (1.288)				0.079ᵃ (6.371)	−0.011 (−1.377)	0.81	19

ᵃSignificant at 1% level or better.
ᵇSignificant at 5% level.

tions on investment in Pennsylvania annually from 1951 through 1969 were regressed on time and various dummy variables in equations (4.2) and (4.3) and on adjusted national investment and various dummies in equations (4.4) and (4.5). For the years 1951 through 1956 the dummy variables were assigned a value of zero. From 1957 through 1969, when the loan program was in operation, the dummies were given a value of one.

The estimates of equations (4.2) and (4.3) suggest that the program shifted down the investment function intercept. This, however, must be interpreted with care. It can only be regarded as the effect of the program if other factors that affect the relationship between state investment and time were held constant. The low values for the $\bar{R}^2$s for these equations make them particularly suspect. Equations (4.4) and (4.5), relating Pennsylvania investment to national investment, perform better as measured by the $\bar{R}^2$s. However, in none of the equations are the coefficients of the dummy variables significantly different from zero at 5 percent. The implicit investment function approach, therefore, suggests that the Pennsylvania program is ineffective.

Induced Investment by Industry. With somewhat mixed evidence of the effect of Pennsylvania's loan program on state investment derived from the explicit and implicit investment function approaches, induced investment by industry over the period 1956-1969 was estimated. The magnitudes are presented in Table 4-6.

Table 4-6
Induced Investment by Industry in Pennsylvania, 1956-1969

SIC Code*	Industry Name	Real Value of Induced Investment (thousands of dollars)
20	Food and kindred products	163,963
21	Tobacco manufactures	15,027
22	Textile mill products	−49,103
23	Apparel and other finished products made from fabrics and similar materials	1,627
24	Lumber and wood products, except furniture	29,005
25	Furniture and fixtures	−151,194
26	Paper and allied products	280,983
27	Printing and publishing and allied industries	32,129
28	Chemicals and allied products	−7,731
30	Rubber and miscellaneous plastics products	92,149
31	Leather and leather products	−20,229
32	Stone, clay, glass, and concrete products	−438,537
33	Primary metal industries	226,152
34	Fabricated metal products, except ordnance machinery and transportation equipment	−143,125
35	Machinery, except electrical	74,328
37	Transportation equipment	225,983
38	Professional, scientific, and instruments; photographic and optical goods; watches and clocks	−108,723
39	Miscellaneous manufacturing industries	141,676
		+364,380

*Standard Industrial Classification

Industry 29, petroleum refining and related industries, has been omitted from the analysis because only two loans were made within the industry over the entire fourteen-year period. Industry 36, electrical machinery equipment and supplies, was omitted for a different reason. While firms within the industry were active participants in the program, our inability to identify an adequate reference region for the industry suggested that inclusion would distort the final results.

Table 4-7
Estimates of Explicit Investment Functions for Kentucky
(Coefficient and t-Statistic)

Equation Form	Intercept	ΔVA_t	ΔVA_{t-1}	ΔVA_{t-2}	ΔVA_{t-3}	L_t	L_{t-1}	L_{t-3}	$\bar{R}^2$	n
4.6	38.585 (1.215)	0.219[b] (2.159)	0.312[a] (3.028)	0.250[b] (2.171)	0.281[b] (2.374)				0.56	22
4.7	55.463[b] (2.457)	0.193[a] (2.716)	0.243[a] (3.292)	0.104 (1.184)	0.141 (1.576)	0.592[b] (2.250)	0.167 (0.577)	0.623[b] (2.480)	0.78	22
4.7	50.364[b] (1.793)	0.200[b] (2.254)	0.289[a] (3.190)	0.165 (1.557)	0.185 (1.682)	0.722[b] (2.516)			0.67	22

[a]Significant at 1% level or better.
[b]Significant at 5% level.

According to the data from Table 4-6, the real value of induced investment over the period was $364 million. This estimate swings the evidence more clearly in favor of the Pennsylvania loan program.

The Kentucky Bond Program

Explicit Investment Function. The explicit investment study for Kentucky yielded uniformly positive results.[g] In this case, the inducement variable entered in the regression was the total amount of revenue bonds floated every year. As with Pennsylvania, an interest rate variable was not included for comparable reasons. In every equation tried, at least one loan (bond) variable had a positive and significant coefficient. The results are shown in Table 4-7. The coefficient or sum of coefficients of the bond variable ranged from 0.72 to 1.22 (when significant).

Because an entire project can be financed by a revenue bond issue, the size of the bond variable coefficient is quite reasonable. It suggests that somewhat less than 100 percent of revenue bond issues created additional investment. A multiplier effect on related investment of 2, for example, would predict that 36 to 61 percent of revenue bonds created additional investment.

In the same manner as Pennsylvania, a dummy variable was entered into the investment equation in place of the bond variable. With Kentucky the zero-one allocation was more difficult, since the program has been in effect since 1951, the earliest year for which time series data were available. Somewhat arbitrarily, years in which total bond issues were less than $12 million were assigned a zero dummy value, while other years were assigned a one. This dummy was positive and highly significant in all equations. This result reinforces the results above.

Implicit Investment Function. The results of application of the implicit investment function somewhat confirm the conclusion from the explicit function. Some of the coefficients of the dummy variables on the intercept and slope are positive and close to signifi-

---

[g]The Kentucky program may in part be more successful than the other programs investigated because the incentive includes a property tax exemption. This is not measured in our equations but it obviously makes the Kentucky package more attractive.

Table 4-8
Estimates of Implicit Investment Functions for Kentucky
(Coefficient and t-Statistic)

Equation Form	Intercept	t	D_t	$D_{t}t$	$I_t^{us} - I_t^j$	$(I_t^{us} - I_t^j)D_t$	$\bar{R}^2$	n
4.2	38.716[b] (1.767)	12.965[a] (7.177)	27.262 (1.059)				.76	22
4.3	39.508[b] (1.835)	12.723[a] (7.125)		2.231 (1.371)			.77	22
4.4	−130.732[a] (−4.546)		3.418 (0.179)		0.026[a] (10.931)		.88	22
4.5	−134.367[a] (−4.506)				0.026[a] (10.539)	−0.000 (−0.185)	.88	22

[a]Significant at 1% level or better.
[b]Significant at 5% level.

cant at 5 percent. The estimates are presented in Table 4-8. Observations on state investment annually from 1951 through 1972 were used. For the years 1963 through 1968, the dummy variables were assigned a value of one, indicating that the program was in operation and total issues exceeded $12 million. For the other years, the dummy variables were given a value of zero.

Again, the $\bar{R}^2$s are higher for the second set of equations; however, the dummy variables are all insignificant in the second set. This suggests that when corrections are made for the changing investment climate nationally, the revenue bond program appears to have no effect on state investment patterns. While this may be the case, it is inconsistent with other evidence that strongly supports the program and may be the result of difficulty in applying the dummy variable model to the Kentucky case, rather than the result of lack of cause and effect. Our inability to collect time series data on investment prior to introduction of the Kentucky program forced us to use the dummy variable counter in a manner different from the other states. While in theory there is nothing wrong with the approach, it simply means that rather than counting the program as beginning in 1951, we counted it as beginning in 1963 after it had reached a certain size, a constraint that was not imposed on the other states. This may have decreased the ability of the dummy variable model to measure the impact of the program, particularly if impacts accumulated through time. In addition, the implicit investment function itself has inherent specification problems. Because of this and the strongly positive evidence of the explicit investment function approach, we conclude that the Kentucky revenue bond program is effective in creating additional investment in the state.

Cost-Benefit Analysis

In the previous sections we examined empirically three programs. Industrial revenue bonds proved to be effective in inducing industry. Loan guarantees were found to have little or no effect on investment. Our results for loan programs, although mixed, provided some evidence that loan programs do bring industrial investment into the states providing them. Our task now is to determine whether these programs are of net benefit to the state. To this end we employ cost-benefit analysis. The following paragraphs briefly outline the procedure but make no attempt to grapple with the numerous strengths and weaknesses of cost-benefit analysis per se.[8]

Measuring Benefits

The total benefits of a financial inducement program are measured by the total income it creates. The inducement occasions investment spending; the construction and operation of new plants or addition to plant provide employment and, of course, wages and salaries for employees. Moreover, there are other benefits in the form of rent and "profits." These payments to factors are spent on goods and services produced internally, spent on goods and services imported from other states, or saved. To the extent that the inducement-occasioned income is spent internally, it becomes income to other people in the state, who, in turn, spend internally, import from other states, or save. The process continues indefinitely, but each round adds a smaller amount to domestic income than the previous round did; savings and imports are the leakages by which total factor payments must be reduced to determine the next round income effect. This, of course, is but a description of the familiar multiplier effect.

If we define β as the marginal propensity to consume internally, we can derive the multiplier for induced investment spending in the state. Each one dollar spending increase initially becomes one dollar of income to the recipient who spends the portion β internally. In the next round β times the $\$\beta$ will be spent. This continues until total spending and income created from the initial one dollar increased spending is (in dollars):

$$1 + \beta + \beta^2 + \beta^3 + \dots + \beta^\infty. \qquad (4.8)$$

Equation (4.8) is an infinite geometric series, which may be summed and rewritten in terms of the familiar multiplier:

$$\frac{1}{(1-\beta)}. \qquad (4.8a)$$

The total income-producing effect of induced investment from an industrial inducement program applied to a situation of unemployment is equation (4.8a) times the amount of induced investment:

$$\Delta Y = \frac{1}{(1-\beta)}\Delta I. \qquad (4.9)$$

The total benefit b_t of a financial inducement program in year t can be measured by the total increase in income it produces in that year:

$$b_t = \frac{1}{(1-\beta)}\Delta I_t. \qquad (4.10)$$

Total present value benefits B_0 of a financial inducement applied over an n year period are:

$$B_0 = \sum_{t=1}^{n}\frac{b_t}{(1+d)^t} = \sum_{t=1}^{n}\frac{1}{(1-\beta)}\frac{\Delta I_t}{(1+d)^t} \qquad (4.11)$$

where d is the "appropriate" rate of discount for the state.

The Discount Rate

The discount rate d must be viewed as an opportunity cost of funds to the state. If the state were to undertake every social investment that has a rate of return greater than or equal to its cost of funds that is—if the state maximizes its net worth—the opportunity cost of funds would be the state's bond rate of interest. This bond rate of interest approximates the lowest possible opportunity cost of state funds. Presumably a financial inducement program would be financed out of taxes or by borrowing. The opportunity cost of taxes is the rate the taxpayers could have earned on the funds if they had been allowed to retain them. The cost of borrowing would, of course, be the tax-exempt interest rate.

If a state rations capital, d may be higher than the bond interest rate i. If a financial inducement program displaces another state investment with social rate of return $r > i$, then the true cost of funds is r. Accordingly, in our computations we use a range of discount rates to be certain that we have encompassed the true discount rate.

Measuring Costs

The costs associated with an inducement program depend on the program. IDBs have only administrative costs—costs incurred by the authority plus imputed costs covering the services of other state agencies, as well as imputed costs representing the services rendered by private individuals, firms, and institutions. Loan guarantee programs have these administrative and imputed costs and, in addition, incur costs for losses, offset to some degree by premium charges. Loan programs carry the cost of the outlays per se, less the repayments, plus administrative costs and costs imputed to other stage agencies and to private interests. These direct and indirect costs we symbolize as C_t.

Inducement program costs are financed largely out of taxes. Even when a program is financed initially from bond issues, the debt service is tax financed. It follows then that the costs will reduce spending. Additional taxes levied on an individual will cause reduced in-state spending, import spending, and savings. Again the taxes are subject to a multiplier effect, negative this time. Total income foregone will be a multiple of the tax levy. The multiplier, however, will not be the usual tax multiplier. The typical tax multiplier measures the net effect on the income stream and thus has a first round value of β, since the reduction in savings, $1-\beta$, does not result in a reduction in total spending. In our context, however, the reduced saving is a cost to the people of the state, and so it must be included in total costs (foregone spending and saving). Thus the first round cost of one dollar in taxes for inducements is one dollar. Note now that spending was reduced by only β in the first round so that the total multiplier would be

$$1 + \beta^2 + \beta^2 + \ldots + \beta^{\infty} = \left(\frac{1}{1-\beta} - \beta\right). \qquad (4.12)$$

The cost multiplier is smaller than the benefit multiplier by β, the marginal propensity to consume internally.[h]

Total cost for year t, c_t, is equal to actual costs times the cost multiplier:

$$c_t = \left(\frac{1}{(1-\beta)} - \beta\right) C_t. \qquad (4.13)$$

Total present value costs, C_0, applied over an n year period are:

$$C_0 = \sum_{t=1}^{n} \frac{c_t}{(1+d)^t} = \sum_{t=1}^{n} \left(\frac{1}{(1-\beta)} - \beta\right) \frac{C_t}{(1+d)^t} \qquad (4.14)$$

Benefit-Cost Ratios

Benefit-cost ratios for an inducement program may now be computed:

$$\frac{B_0}{C_0} = \frac{\sum_{t=1}^{n} \frac{1}{(1-\beta)} \frac{\Delta I_t}{(1+d)^t}}{\sum_{t=1}^{n} \left(\frac{1}{(1-\beta)} - \beta\right) \frac{C_t}{(1+d)^t}}. \qquad (4.15)$$

The multiplier in the denominator is smaller than that in the numerator. We can be conservative in our estimates by using $1/(1-\beta)$ as the multiplier for both numerator and denominator. This overstates costs and therefore understates benefit-cost ratios but allows us to eliminate multipliers by cancellation and simplify:

$$\frac{B_0}{C_0} = \frac{\sum_{t=1}^{n} \frac{\Delta I_t}{(1+d)^t}}{\sum_{t=1}^{n} \frac{C_t}{(1+d)^t}}. \qquad (4.16)$$

Loan Programs. Above we estimated $\hat{\alpha}_1$ for the Pennsylvania pro-

[h] The normal tax multiplier would be $\beta/(1-\beta)$, which is equal to the spending multiplier minus one.

gram by two forms of explicit investment equation (4.7). $\alpha_1 L_t$ from the first form and $\hat{\alpha}_1 L_{t-1}$ from the second form of equation (4.7) (Table 4-4) provide estimates of induced investment since

$$\hat{\alpha}_1 = \frac{\partial I_t}{\partial L_t} \quad \text{or} \quad \frac{\partial I_t}{\partial L_{t-1}} . \tag{4.17}$$

We need only apply the $\hat{\alpha}_1$ coefficients to actual amounts lent and discount their products to determine benefits for Pennsylvania (multipliers not applied). Tables 4-9 and 4-10 show the appropriate computations.

Table 4-11 gives benefit-cost ratios using the benefits calculated above and discounted costs for discount rates of 3, 6, 9, and 12 percent. The discounted costs consist of administrative and direct lending costs. Estimates of administrative costs are those made by Sazama.[9] Lending costs are calculated by: (1) discounting repayments on loans made in any year t back to year t using the applicable discount rate; (2) subtracting discounted repayments from the loan amount in each year to yield a net loan cost; and (3) discounting net loan cost in each year back to the base year (1957).

Since our range of discount rate (3-12 percent) is higher than the Pennsylvania lending rate of 2 percent, the net loan cost will be positive—that is, Pennsylvania loses money with each loan made because it lends at less than its cost of capital. These lending costs increase as the discount rate is increased, causing total costs to increase with the discount rate.

The Pennsylvania benefit-cost ratios are large at any of the above discount rates. They would be even larger, of course, if we had applied the regional multipliers. It will nevertheless be recalled that a dummy variable approach cast some doubt on the $\hat{\alpha}_1$ coefficients used in the above computations. The interindustry approach, however, also showed positive induced investment but not of the magnitude of either of the sums in Tables 4-9 and 4-10. As a precautionary check, then, we may reduce our benefits by noting that the overstatement of induced investment, at maximum, is $1,737,866/ $364,380, or 4.77 times. (Figures are from Tables 4-6 and 4-9.) The denominator is real induced investment measured for individual industries. Reducing the lowest benefit-cost ratio by dividing it by this factor still yields a ratio far greater than unity, indicating that the program is of net benefit.[i]

[i] Putting the numerator in real terms (index-1967 = 100) would increase the factor somewhat but would not bring any of the already conservative ratios down to one.

Table 4-9
Discounted Benefits: Pennsylvania Loan Program, $\hat{\alpha}_1 = 10.91$

t	Year	Loan Amount L_t (thousands of dollars)	$\Delta I(\hat{\alpha}_1, L_t)$ (thousands of dollars)	Discounted Benefits			
				$d = 3\%$	$d = 6\%$	$d = 9\%$	$d = 12\%$
1	1957	1,255	13,692				
2	1958	2,293	25,017				
3	1959	2,856	31,159				
4	1960	3,903	42,582				
5	1961	5,085	55,477				
6	1962	4,976	54,288				
7	1963	9,798	106,896				
8	1964	11,569	126,218				
9	1965	10,500	114,555				
10	1966	28,382	309,648				
11	1967	18,138	197,886				
12	1968	31,672	345,542				
13	1969	28,864	314,906				
			$1,737,866	$1,301,049	$989,400	$763,889	$598,479

Table 4-10
Discounted Benefits: Pennsylvania Loan Program, $\hat{\alpha}_1 = 11.76$

				Discounted Benefits		
t	Year	Loan Amount (L_{t-1}) (thousands of dollars)	$\Delta I(\hat{\alpha}_1, L_{t-1})$ (thousands of dollars)	$d = 3\%$	$d = 6\%$	$d = 9\%$	$d = 12\%$
1	1957	0	0				
2	1958	1,255	14,759				
3	1959	2,293	26,966				
4	1960	2,856	33,587				
5	1961	3,903	45,989				
6	1962	5,085	59,800				
7	1963	4,976	58,518				
8	1964	9,798	115,224				
9	1965	11,569	136,051				
10	1966	10,500	123,480				
11	1967	28,382	333,772				
12	1968	18,138	213,303				
13	1969	31,672	372,463				
			$1,533,912	$1,136,390	$855,983	$653,840	$506,532

Table 4-11
Benefit-Cost Ratios: Pennsylvania Loan Program

	Discount Rate			
	3%	*6%*	*9%*	*12%*
$\hat{\alpha}_1 = 10.91$	$\dfrac{1,301,049}{12,393} = 105.0$	$\dfrac{989,400}{29,899} = 33.1$	$\dfrac{763,889}{35,744} = 21.4$	$\dfrac{598,479}{35,758} = 16.7$
$\hat{\alpha}_1 = 11.76$	$\dfrac{1,136,390}{12,393} = 91.7$	$\dfrac{855,983}{29,899} = 29.0$	$\dfrac{653,840}{35,744} = 18.3$	$\dfrac{506,532}{35,758} = 14.1$

Loan Guarantees. It will be recalled that most of our regressions indicated that no net investment was induced by the Connecticut loan guarantee program. But there were costs—the actual administrative costs of the authority and service costs imputed to other state agencies and to private individuals and firms. Hence the benefit-cost ratio is zero. The program causes a net loss to the state. Even if we use the interindustry model induced investment figures, which totaled $136,000, the benefit-cost ratios must still be less than unity, since administrative and imputed costs for the same five-year period were $160,000. A benefit-cost ratio less than one indicates a net loss to the state.

IDB Programs. Here the evidence is positive. The benefits in any year in Kentucky are conservatively estimated to be[j]

$$0.72 \text{ (\$Amount of Bonds Issued)} \frac{1}{(1-\beta)} \ .$$

The benefit-cost ratio is clearly some very large number. Assuming the program cost $50,000 to administer each year (a one-year high for Connecticut), one bond alone of less than $100,000 would create benefits in excess of costs. There can be no question about the efficacy of an industrial revenue bond program.[k]

---

[j] Again, benefits are computed by multiplying the regression coefficient (Table 4-7) times the program variable to measure induced investment and multiplying the result by the regional multipliers.

[k] It should be noted, however, that the Kentucky measurement was, for the most part, for a period during which IDB issues were unlimited. The effect may not be as great under existing laws.

Impacts on Neighboring States

One final question of interest is whether those inducement programs that are effective have damaging impacts on neighboring states that do not offer comparable programs. In order to examine this question empirically, it is necessary to identify a state that, based on our analysis, has an effective program and has a neighboring state that is similar in competitive position except for an inducement program. Pennsylvania, with what appears to be a successful loan program, and its neighbor New Jersey were chosen. New Jersey had no inducement program prior to 1974, borders on only three states, primarily Pennsylvania, and offers industry locational advantages similar to those of Pennsylvania.

At least some of the evidence presented above indicates that the Pennsylvania loan program caused manufacturing investment to be made in that state that would not have been made in the program's absence. Pennsylvania's success does not necessarily pose a threat to New Jersey, however; there is no compelling reason to believe that New Jersey had been hurt because of investment induced in Pennsylvania. Here we examine whether the Pennsylvania loan program has been a factor in New Jersey's decrease in number of manufacturing firms in recent years. Rather than focus on investment, however, we concentrate on the impact on jobs.

The Model

If the net savings from a low-interest loan are large enough, a firm can be expected to locate where the cheap loan is offered rather than at an alternative location that might otherwise minimize costs. This assumes that variations in market potential are not significant between the locations and that the firm can estimate its long-run alternative costs with a large degree of certainty. Of course, if other costs of doing business also favor a firm's move to the area granting cheap loans, it may be difficult to say whether the loans were the cause of firm relocations. The assumption with regard to market demand would seem reasonable for New Jersey locations vis-à-vis at least those in eastern Pennsylvania.

Previous evidence indicated that the Pennsylvania program

caused state investment spending to increase, suggesting that employment would also increase.[1] However, employment patterns are changing in the United States, and Pennsylvania's employment as a ratio of U.S. employment can be expected to display a trend of industry out-migration. Hence, the simplest hypothesis to test is that Pennsylvania's percentage of total U.S. manufacturing employment displays a direct relationship to PIDA loans and, at the same time, an industry migration trend reflecting changes in any number of non-loan related locational variables. This would confirm our previous evidence.

The corollary hypothesis is that New Jersey's manufacturing employment percentage should show an inverse relationship to the PIDA loans if it loses employment to its neighbor as a result of the program. New Jersey employment should also be affected by an industry migration trend similar to Pennsylvania's since it may also be considered an old industrial state relative to the rest of the United States.

To test these hypotheses we estimated the following equation for both Pennsylvania and New Jersey:

$$(N_j/N_{us})_t = \alpha_0 + \alpha_1 L_t + \alpha_2 t \qquad (4.18)$$

where $(N_j/N_{us})_t$ = state share of U.S. manufacturing employment in year t, and L_t = amount lent by Pennsylvania in year t.

Note that this form is similar to the implicit investment function approach, using time as a proxy for all location factors other than the loan program. This time, however, the dependent variable is an employment share, rather than an absolute amount of investment. Thus, the implicit nature of the specification might be expected to perform better.

The Results

The estimated equations are presented in Table 4-12.[m] The New Jersey equation covering the period 1956-1971 is presented first and

---

[1] Presumably a plant alteration could reduce the total need for labor if it incorporated improved technology. However, before a loan is approved, PIDA requires that the firm give an estimate of the additional number of jobs that will be created.

[m] The Cochran-Orcutt fully iterative regression technique was used to estimate the coefficients. Unless otherwise indicated, results mentioned as "significant" were statistically significant at the 5 percent level.

Table 4-12
Estimates of Manufacturing Employment Share Regression
(Coefficient and t-Statistic)

State	Time Period	Pennsylvania Loans (millions of dollars)	Time	Intercept Dummy	Slope Dummy	Interest Rate	R^2	Estimated Employment Change
New Jersey	1956-71	−0.02 (−2.13)	−0.00085 (−5.77)				0.98	−71,000
Pennsylvania	1947-64	0.30 (4.75)	−0.0013 (−26.37)				0.98	250,000
Pennsylvania	1947-69	0.18 (6.15)	−0.0012 (−26.34)				0.98	540,000
Pennsylvania	1956-71	0.18 (3.03)	−0.0011 (−8.27)	0.0056 (3.12)		−0.00081 (−1.84)	0.94	670,000
Pennsylvania	1956-71	0.17 (3.03)	−0.0010 (−8.46)		0.00000041 (3.15)	−0.00089 (−1.95)	0.94	670,000

indicates that the state lost manufacturing jobs because of the Pennsylvania program. As hypothesized, the Pennsylvania loan variable has a negative and significant coefficient. The estimated employment change due to the program is calculated and presented in the last column.

The results covering the loan program period 1956-1971 at first seemed to indicate that the program had no effect on Pennsylvania manufacturing employment. The poor results for our time period seemed to conflict with those obtained by Gold for the period 1947-1964.[10] When we repeated Gold's experiment we reproduced his result—evidence of a large gain in manufacturing employment from the loans. This led us to believe that the effect of the recession of 1969-1970 had caused our statistical relationship for 1956-1971 to be misspecified since the results for the prerecession years were positive and statistically significant.[n] We therefore respecified the relationship to include terms representing the 1969-1970 recession. This time the effect of the loan program appeared to be positive and significant over the entire span of years. We implicitly included the 1969-1970 recession in the 1956-1971 analysis by adding intercept and slope dummies for the time variable. An explicit interest rate variable was also included. The coefficient for the loan program became significant and of approximately the same value as the prerecession coefficients.[o]

Thus, the Pennsylvania data show evidence of a large employment gain in the total manufacturing sector as a result of the loans prior to the 1969-1970 recession and somewhat less convincing evidence of a gain from the loans when the recession period is added. The Pennsylvania and New Jersey results are consistent.

The evidence presented suggests that Pennsylvania loans may be

[n]The loan coefficients are significant at the 5 percent level and an autocorrelation problem suggested in the earlier equations is eliminated. The number of jobs estimated is apparently too large, however, since the coefficients indicate that 250,000-540,000 jobs were created in a total manufacturing work force of about 1.5 million. Our formulation differs somewhat from the Gold formulation, which tends to be dominated by cyclical changes. Our results, nevertheless, are virtually the same as his, in this case at least. Both our formulation and Gold's, however, have used a loan series that is unadjusted for price changes. This means that there may be some degree of bias in the loan coefficient. The bias may be reflected in the estimated employment effects which are "too large."

[o]Once more, however, the Durbin-Watson coefficients were in the indeterminate range indicating a possible autocorrelation problem. And once again the indicated employment increase of over 600,000 seems far too high.

Dummy variables and the interest rate were not necessary in the New Jersey equation, showing a reduction in employment share. When entered, the coefficients were insignificant while the loan coefficient was unaffected.

aggravating the New Jersey unemployment problem. If this is the general impact of inducements on neighboring states, there are three courses of possible action: (1) each state could act in self-defense by inaugurating similar programs; (2) states could negotiate interstate agreements to coordinate industrial inducement policies; or (3) states could appeal to Congress to make such programs illegal. We discuss this last issue in our concluding chapter.

5 Microeconomic Analysis of Program Efficiency

With the estimates of aggregate impacts of industrial inducement programs as background, we move to a microeconomic analysis of program efficiency. Here we are concerned with whether there are industry differences in response to inducement schemes and whether such differences can be explained by industry characteristics. Thus, the focus is on the industrial composition of participating investment. Characteristics of firms that participate can be evaluated with respect to area development potential, and the geographic distribution of participants within a state can be compared with the geographic distribution of growth or employment problems.

This kind of analysis cannot be done with the induced investment estimates since the location of the investment within the state is undefined. In addition, second- and later-round inducements depend as much on industry linkages as on the design of the inducement program. Without estimates of first-round investment induced alone, we rely on participating investment for our analysis. However, it should be noted that participating investment does not necessarily represent net induced investment. The investment might have taken place in the absence of the program, or may replace investment by another firm or another industry. Nevertheless, analysis of participants can suggest at least first-round impacts. The information gained by examining participant characteristics is most useful if applied to a successful program type, such as a loan program or, more clearly, a revenue bond program. For this reason we chose to evaluate participants in a revenue bond program. The Massachusetts program was selected because of the relatively better availability of Standard Metropolitan Statistical Area (SMSA) data in New England as compared to other areas of the country. Of the five New England states with bond programs, only Massachusetts has issued an appreciable amount. None of the three states with a loan program has used it extensively. Finally, unlike the Pennsylvania loan program, the percentage of project cost subsidized by the program does not depend on area unemployment rates. Thus the intrastate location decision of the participating firm is not constrained by the program.

The Massachusetts revenue bond program is typical. Eligible expenditures include those for land, building, improvements, machinery, and equipment for manufacturing and related warehousing facilities. A property tax exemption is not granted to the participating firm. From its start in 1967 through 1973, there have been twenty-one bond issues approved for a total of $42.9 million. It is assumed, based on our previous evidence, that the program resulted in net increases in state investment. The question is whether it was in the right industries and in the right places. Unless idle funds are available, the bonds have an opportunity cost, and investment elsewhere is sacrificed. Therefore it is important that the program be applied selectively. It is interesting to note, however, that, from a state's viewpoint, investment sacrificed in other states is immaterial.

General Characteristics of the Firms

The twenty-one bond recipients are classified by two-digit SIC code in Table 5-1. Even with the broad classes of Table 5-1, these bond recipients are grouped in thirteen categories. There is some concentration within electrical and nonelectrical machinery. Seven of the issues went to companies in two closely related groups (one company manufactures both electrical and nonelectrical machinery). The concentration is not surprising since machinery manufacture is capital intensive and a revenue bond represents a capital subsidy. In addition, machinery manufacture is an area in which Massachusetts has had an apparent comparative advantage.

Of the companies that participated in the program, all were well established; none was a new venture. The Massachusetts Department of Commerce and Development, in order to facilitate sale of the bond issue, requires that the firms have a respectable financial record, a requirement that apparently precludes new ventures from participating. It is possible, therefore, that in the absence of the use of general obligation bonds backed by the municipalities, a loan program for greater credit risks may be necessary to encourage new concerns.

Table 5-1
Number of Bond Recipients by Two-Digit SIC Code

SIC Classification	Number of Companies
20 Food and kindred products	2
23 Apparel and related products	1
25 Furniture and fixtures	1
26 Paper and allied products	1
28 Chemicals and allied products	1
30 Rubber and plastic products, not elsewhere classified	1
31 Leather and leather products	1
33 Primary metals	1
35 Machinery, except electrical	3
36 Electrical machinery	4
37 Transportation equipment	2
50 Wholesale trade: durable goods	2
51 Wholesale trade: nondurable goods	1

Development Potential of the Firms

Employment Generated

The primary objective of the bond program is to increase employment. When a community seeks state approval of a bond issue, it must be justified by high local unemployment rates or the threat of high unemployment rates. The bond issues combined raised about $43 million, which created 4,713 jobs. Of the twenty-one issues, seventeen were for new plants for established firms, two were for additions to existing plants, and two were for renovation or renewal. Table 5-2 shows the number of new jobs and the corresponding amount of bond issues. The value of the bond issue per new employee gives a measure of program effectiveness. Site value was excluded from the calculations:[a] $V = p/n$ where V = capitalized payments per employee attributable to bond issue, less site value; p = amount of the bond issue, less site value; and n = new employment.

The last column of Table 5-2 shows the bond issue, or payments,

[a] Not all firms purchased land. If site value were not subtracted, ceteris paribus established plants would be favored over new plants.

Table 5-2
Bonds Issues, by Dollar Value, and Employment Generated

Bond Length (years)	Amount	Site Value	Plant and Equipment	Number New Employees	Capitalized Value Per Employee
10	$ 800,000	$ 66,000	$ 734,000	150	$ 4,893
15	500,000	77,500	422,500	75	5,633
15	480,000		480,000	105	4,571
20	2,100,000	271,400	1,828,600	300	6,095
10	1,500,000	18,000	1,482,000	200	7,410
5	1,000,000	483,000	517,000	200	2,585
20	3,500,000	301,668	3,198,332	130	24,603
20	175,000	50,000	125,000	11	11,364
20	2,400,000	36,000	2,364,000	327	7,229
12	600,000	66,000	534,000	35	15,267
15	350,000	70,000	280,000	50	5,600
20	995,000	23,000	972,000	100	9,720
25	12,000,000	1,536,000	10,464,000	2,000	5,232
22	1,000,000	125,000	875,000	50	17,500
15	1,150,000	175,000	975,000	148	6,588
30	10,000,000	1,300,000	8,700,000	250	34,800
10	462,000	50,000	412,000	42	9,810
5	1,500,000	866,439	633,561	150	4,224
15	401,290		401,290	40	10,032
20	1,000,000	40,000	960,000	300	3,200
15	995,590		995,590	50	19,912
	$42,908,880	$5,555,007	$37,353,873	4,713	$ 7,926

Source: Massachusetts Department of Commerce and Development.

per new new employee. The mean value is $7,926 per new job, with a range of $2,585 to $34,800. Crepas and Stevenson suggest a maximum expenditure of $16,000 per new employee.[1] Using this criterion, about 75 percent of the bond issues were effective; only four issues bought jobs at too great an expense in terms of capital required to support the jobs.

Department of Commerce Ratings

The U.S. Department of Commerce has rated four-digit manufacturing industries according to their potential for area development using data from the 1958, 1963, and 1967 *Census of Manufactures*. Ratings are based on six characteristics of the industry. Assuming

Table 5-3
Grading of Manufacturing Firms

Company	SIC Code*	Growth Rating	Long-Term Growth Trend	Capital Formation	Average Wage Rate	Percent Blue Collar	Labor Intensity
1	3651	VHG	HG	VH	M	M	M
	3585	HG	HG	VH	H	M	M
	3679	VHG	VHG	VH	L	M	M
2	3362	MG	HG	M	M	M	M
3	3651	VHG	HG	VH	M	M	M
4	2531	MG	HG	M	L	M	M
5	3621	MG	MG	M	M	M	M
6	2652	D	D	VL	L	H	H
7	2335	S	S	NA	L	H	H
8	3642	MG	HG	H	M	M	M
9	3531	MG	MG	H	H	M	M
10	3732	MG	MG	L	L	H	H
11	3573	VHG	VHG	VH	M	VL	M
12	2087	S	HG	M	M	L	VL
13	2013	S	MG	H	M	M	M
14	2893	MG	S	M	M	L	L
15	3079	VHG	VHG	VH	L	M	M
16	3679	VHG	VHG	VH	L	M	M
17	3131	D	D	NA	L	H	H

VHG: Very high growth   VH: Very high   L: Low
HG: High growth   H: High   VL: Very low
MG: Moderate growth   M: Moderate   NA: Not available
  S: Static growth
  D: Declining growth

*Standard Industrial Classification Code.

Source: U.S. Department of Commerce, "Growth and Labor Characteristics of Manufacturing Industries." *Census of Manufactures* (1972).

Table 5-4
Four-Digit SIC Code Definitions

Code	Definitions
2013	Sausages and other prepared meat products
2087	Flavoring extracts, not elsewhere classified
2335	Women's and children's dresses
2531	Public building furniture
2652	Setup paperboard boxes
2893	Printing ink
3079	Miscellaneous plastic products
3131	Footwear cut stock
3362	Brass, bronze, copper castings
3531	Construction machinery
3573	Computer machinery
3585	Refrigeration machinery
3621	Motors and generators
3642	Lighting fixtures
3651	Radio and TV receiving sets
3679	Electronic components, not elsewhere classified
3732	Boat building and repairing
3751	Motorcycles, bicycles, and parts
5051	Metals service centers and offices
5149	Groceries and related products, not elsewhere classified

Source: Executive Office of the President, Office of Management and Budget, *Standard Industrial Classification Manual* (Washington, D.C.: Government Printing Office, 1972).

that firms which participated in the Massachusetts program are similar to the average for their four-digit industry, we can assess the development potential of each of the manufacturing participants. The information is presented in Table 5-3. Industry definitions are given in Table 5-4.

The first characteristic is growth, measured by the ratio of the average annual employment in 1966-1967 to that in 1958-1960. Of the seventeen manufacturing firms listed, only five displayed stagnant or declining growth nationally.[b] These five are in textile, food processing, paper, and leather-goods industries, areas of manufacture in which Massachusetts once specialized but where the state has been losing its share of employment over the postwar years. Although in stagnant or declining industries, these firms may demand relatively large amounts of labor at a fairly low skill level, absorbing the kinds of workers likely to be suffering severe unemployment in the state.

The second relevant characteristic is long-term growth potential

[b]Three of the issues went to distributors. Company 2 received two issues. Company 1 corresponds to three SIC codes.

as measured by the ratio of industry value added to the all-manufacturing average for 1967. Using this as a criterion, four companies show stagnant or declining trends. Three of these also show stagnant or declining employment growth. The fourth is a firm in the printing industry, which has medium employment growth and has been declining in importance in Massachusetts in recent years.

The next criterion is the amount of capital formation, measured by gross value of depreciable assets in the industry in 1967 compared with 1963. This index is highly correlated with the employment growth criterion. Not surprisingly, six of the seventeen companies listed fall into industries classified as very high in capital formation; five of these are in machinery manufacture. But capital formation per se is not especially desirable. While it does mean increased property tax revenue to communities, this is not a stated goal of the program. The purpose of the program is to provide jobs and income, and income to capital is likely to flow out of the community. Capital formation is desirable if accompanied by employment growth and especially if it represents increased demand for the kinds of labor that are unemployed.

The average wage rate of production workers is the next index of development potential. Ceteris paribus a high average wage is desirable. However, a high wage is likely to mean a high skill level. If the unemployed in the community have low skills, then the appropriate kind of firm to induce is one that employs such labor and therefore pays relatively low wages. Bringing the job to match the labor force must be the justification for any industrial incentive scheme. Unemployment in areas of surplus labor cannot be removed by a reduction of the wage rate to the extent that it is inflexible downward. Therefore, in the absence of labor migration, area investment must increase, thereby increasing the demand for labor and relieving unemployment. But benefits will be enjoyed only if demand is increased for the kind of labor that is unemployed, since frictions on the supply side of the labor market mean that one kind of labor is not readily converted into another. In the aggregate, if this is not how the programs work, then they serve only to shift jobs from one place to another, even state to state, without increasing total employment.[2] If, on the other hand, only medium- to high-wage jobs are wanted, then a program to provide jobs for medium and highly skilled labor is required. In such a case, training subsidies would seem appropriate.[3]

The average production wage rate is a rough indicator of skill level. In 1974, craftsmen earned an average of $10,972, operators $7,800, and nonfarm laborers $7,748.[4] It is also generally true that unemployment decreases with increased skill level. In 1974, average national unemployment rates were 4.3 percent for craftsmen, 6.8 percent for operators, and 10.1 percent for nonfarm laborers.[5] Thus if the industry has a high production wage rate, it would likely require highly skilled labor, a group less likely to be unemployed. To attract employees, the firm would either compete for the existing local labor pool via an increased wage rate, import employees from other areas, or train unskilled workers. Only the last alternative is a direct and primary benefit to the community, and it may have limited potential. Whatever the outcome, although there are possibilities for spillover or roll-out effects, the community would be fighting unemployment indirectly and/or inefficiently. For this reason an average wage rating of moderate or low is more desirable from the community's viewpoint, *if the goal is to decrease unemployment*. From Table 5-3 we see that only two industries do not fit this standard, and one of those is part of a multi-industry listing for one company. It is, however, a high or very high growth industry.

The next industry characteristic considered is the percentage of blue-collar workers. In terms of decreasing local unemployment, a high rather than a low percentage of blue-collar workers is desirable because unemployment rates for white-collar workers are generally lower. In 1974, the average male white-collar unemployment rate was 2.2 percent while the blue-collar rate was 6.0 percent.[6] Because blue-collar workers need less formal education, it is easier to fit an unemployed worker into a blue-collar job. While none of the industries listed received a very high blue-collar rating, only three were low or very low. The very low rating is associated with a very high-growth industry, computer machinery manufacture. The two low ratings were received by industries that by some measure displayed stagnant growth. On the other hand, three of the four industries receiving a high blue-collar rating showed declining or stagnant growth by all three growth measures.[c] These four also had low average wage rates. Low wages and high blue-collar percentages within stagnant or declining industries illustrate a basic problem

---

[c] For two industries a capital formation measure was not available, which itself suggests stagnation or decline.

with the use of industrial incentive programs to solve area unemployment: to provide immediate jobs to the unemployed often
means bringing in industries with little growth potential or even
"staying power."

The last criterion considered is the labor intensity of the industry, measured by production worker wages as a percentage of value
added in 1967. Again, since the purpose of the program is to provide
local jobs to unemployed labor, high labor intensity ratings are
preferable. Only four industries received such a rating; three of
these are no-growth industries. The trade-off discussed above is
therefore demonstrated again. Most of the industries received a
moderate rating. Not surprisingly, the high labor intensity industries
are those with low capital formation ratings.

Geographic Distribution of Participants

Another major question concerning the development potential of
any inducement program is the participation by communities. Did
investment take place in the right places (those areas of the state that
needed the jobs)? The 21 bond issues were sponsored by eleven
communities in the state. Six of the bond issues, accounting for more
than half of the total value issued, were sponsored by one community.

Table 5-5 presents information concerning the growth profiles of
the participating communities. Change in value added by manufacture for 1963-1967 is used as a growth measure. The bond program
began in 1967. Since data are not available on a community basis,
SMSA data are used as a proxy. Table 5-5 gives the number of bond
issues by SMSA and the corresponding SMSA growth rates. For
comparison, national average growth rates, mean and median, for
237 SMSAs are presented. It is clear that the growth in value added
in all of the participating SMSAs is below the national average.
However, Marlborough, with the highest growth among participating SMSAs and close to the highest in the state, sponsored the
largest number of issues. The lowest ranked SMSAs, New Bedford
and Fall River, each had only one issue. New Bedford attracted a
dress manufacturer (SIC 2335), a stagnant industry nationally, with
low wages, a large percentage of blue-collar workers, and labor

Table 5-5
Bond Issues by SMSA and SMSA Growth Rate

Location Of Company Receiving Bond	SMSA	SMSA 1963-1967 Change in Value Added by Manufacture	Number of Bond Issues
Hopkinton	None		2
Hudson	None		1
Mansfield	None		2
Framingham	Boston	37.9	1
Walpole	Boston	37.9	2
Brockton	Brockton	30.4	2
Leominster	Fitchburg-Leominster	22.3	2
Dartmouth	New Bedford	8.6	1
Fall River	Fall River	6.2	1
Marlborough	Marlborough	38.9	6
Westfield	Springfield	37.2	1
No Company	Lawrence-Haverhill	19.2	0
No Company	Pittsfield	39.0	0
No Company	Worcester	40.1	0
Mean 237 SMSAs		66.6	
Median 237 SMSAs		39.1	

Source: *County and City Data Book 1972* (U.S. Department of Commerce).

Table 5-6
Employment Trends in Manufacturing Industry: Massachusetts Cities

Location	Average Annual Percentage Change in Total Employment, 1963-1967	Number of Bond Issues
Brockton	−9.3	2
Leominster	4.3	2
Fall River	−8.0	1
Marlborough	25.0	6
Westfield	11.4	1
Lawrence	11.3	0
Pittsfield	4.5	0
Worcester	1.1	0
Mean 36 cities (with 25,000 or more population)	7.1	
Range 36 cities	−16.7 to 58.4	

Source: *County and City Data Book 1972* (U.S. Department of Commerce).

intensive. Fall River lured a boatbuilding and repairing firm (SIC 3732) within a low wage, high blue-collar, and labor-intensive industry. The growth prospects are medium to low.

Table 5-6 supplements Table 5-5 by providing employment growth figures by city for 1963-1967 and the number of bond issues by city. Table 5-6 is based on data for Massachusetts cities with 25,000 inhabitants or more, rather than SMSAs, which explains the discrepancies in coverage between the two tables. Notice that while in only two instances did the employment growth in a bond issue city exceed the thirty-six-city average, seven of the bond issues went to these two cities and six of them went to a city with more than three times the state average growth.

Possibly more important than lack of growth as a criterion for industrial inducement is the presence of an unemployment problem, although the two situations may merge. To examine the unemployment rate by city, SMSA data again had to be used as a proxy. In order to measure the severity of the unemployment problem, SMSA unemployment was measured relative to the state rate, since the question we are concerned with is the distribution of participants within the state according to relative need. Table 5-7 presents SMSA unemployment index on a monthly basis during the period of the revenue bond programs. The Boston data are difficult to interpret since the SMSA encompasses such a large area. None of the three issues received by that SMSA went to the central city. For the rest of the recipient SMSAs, unemployment in most months was higher than the state average, indicating relative need. Again, the most serious problem areas appear to be Fall River and New Bedford where only two issues were approved. Unfortunately, unemployment data during the period of the bond issues are not available for Marlborough.

Conclusions

While our microeconomic analysis was confined to one program in one state, the results are likely to be similar for the other programs used elsewhere, if program recipients are not restricted. Each of the programs is a capital subsidy program of one sort or another and is therefore going to result in the same kind of trade-off problem that we discovered in Massachusetts.

In particular, with respect to industries, there appears to be a

Table 5-7
Monthly Unemployment Index by SMSA [a]

Number of Bond Issues	SMSA	Jan.	Feb.	March	April	May	June	July	Aug.	Sept.	Oct.	Nov.	Dec.
3	Boston												
	1967	0.9	0.9	0.8	0.9	1.1	0.8	0.7	0.8	0.8	0.9	0.8	0.9
	1968	0.8	0.8	0.8	0.8	0.8	0.8	0.8	0.8	0.8	0.9	0.7	0.8
	1969	0.8	0.8	0.8	0.8	1.0	0.7	0.7	0.8	0.8	0.9	0.8	0.8
	1970	0.8	0.8	0.8	0.8	0.8	0.9	0.8	0.8	0.8	0.8	0.8	0.8
	1971	0.8	0.8	0.8	0.8	0.9	0.9	0.8	0.8	0.9	0.9	0.8	0.9
	1972	0.8	0.8	0.8	0.8	0.8	0.9[b]	0.8	0.9	0.9	0.9	0.9	0.8[b]
	1973	0.9	0.8	0.9	0.9[b]	0.9	0.9	0.9	0.9	0.9	0.9	0.9	0.8
2	Brockton												
	1967	1.1	1.1	1.1	1.1	1.2	1.2	1.2	1.0	1.1	1.1	1.1,	1.0
	1968	1.1	1.1	1.1	1.1	1.1	1.0	1.2	1.0	1.0	0.9	0.9	0.9
	1969	1.1	1.1	1.1	1.0	1.1	1.2	1.2	1.1	1.1	1.0	1.1	1.1
	1970	1.1	1.2	1.2	1.2	1.0	1.2	1.2	1.2	1.2	1.1[c]	1.1	1.2
	1971	1.2	1.2	1.2	1.2	1.4	1.2	1.3	1.2	1.2	1.2	1.3	1.2
	1972	1.2	1.3	1.2	1.3	1.0	1.1	1.1	1.2	1.1	1.1	1.2	1.2
	1973	1.2	1.3	1.3	1.3	1.3	1.3	1.4	1.3	1.4	1.3	1.3	1.3
2	Fitchburg-Leominster												
	1967	1.5	1.3	1.5	1.4	1.5	1.5	1.4	1.3	1.4	1.3	1.3	1.4
	1968	1.4	1.3	1.4	1.5	1.5	1.5	1.5	1.5	1.4	1.5	1.5	1.5
	1969	1.5	1.4	1.4	1.5	1.4	1.4	1.4	1.4	1.4	1.3	1.3	1.3
	1970	1.4	1.4	1.5	1.3	1.3	1.3	1.3	1.3	1.4	1.2	1.2	1.4
	1971	1.4	1.4	1.3	1.3	1.4	1.4	1.4	1.4	1.4	1.8	1.4	1.4
	1972	1.4	1.4	1.4	1.3	1.3	1.3	1.3	1.3	0.9	0.9	1.3	1.3
	1973	1.2	1.2	1.1	1.0	1.0	1.0	1.1	1.0	1.0	1.0	1.0	1.1[c]

1	New Bedford											
	1967						Not Available					
	1968						Not Available					
	1969	1.4	1.4	1.7	1.5	1.4	2.1	1.4	1.5	1.5	1.5	1.6	1.6
	1970	1.8	1.6	1.9	1.9	1.7	1.7	1.4	1.7	1.8	1.7	1.7	1.7
	1971	1.8	1.7	1.7	1.4	1.2	1.5	1.1	1.0	1.0	1.0	1.2	1.3
	1972	1.3	1.4	1.3	1.3	1.2	1.3	1.1	1.0	1.0	1.0	1.0	1.1
	1973	1.2	1.2	1.0ᵇ	1.4	1.1	1.3	0.9	1.0	0.9	1.0	1.0	1.0

1	Fall River											
	1967	1.7	1.6	1.6	1.3	1.2	2.2	1.3	1.0	1.3	1.1	1.4	1.5
	1968	1.6	1.4	1.5	1.1	1.1	2.1	1.1	1.0	1.0	1.1	1.3	1.5
	1969	1.7	1.6	1.7	1.3	1.1	2.4	1.3	1.1	1.3	1.2	1.4	1.7
	1970	2.0	1.7	1.6	1.5	1.4	1.4ᵇ	1.1	1.1	1.0	1.0	1.3	1.3
	1971	1.4	1.3	1.3	1.1	1.1	1.1	1.1	0.9	0.9	1.0	1.1	1.1
	1972	1.3	1.3	1.3	1.1	1.2	1.2	1.1	0.9	0.9	1.8	1.2	1.3
	1973	1.2	1.2	1.2	1.1	1.1	1.2	1.0	0.9	0.9	1.1	1.2	1.3

1	Springfield											
	1967	1.0	1.0	1.1	1.2	1.2	1.1	1.1	1.1	1.1	1.1	1.1	1.1
	1968	1.1	1.1	1.2	1.2	1.3	1.2	1.3	1.2	1.3ᵇ	1.2	1.1	1.1
	1969	1.1	1.1	1.2	1.2	1.3	1.1	1.3	1.3	1.3	1.1	1.2	1.2
	1970	1.2	1.1	1.2	1.4	1.3	1.2	1.3	1.2	1.1	1.1	1.1	1.1
	1971	1.2	1.2	1.2	1.3	1.3	1.2	1.3	1.2	1.2	1.2	1.2	1.2
	1972	1.1	1.1	1.2	1.2	1.1	1.1	1.1	1.1	1.1	1.1	1.1	1.0
	1973	1.0	1.0	1.1	1.0	1.2	0.9	1.0	1.2	0.9	1.1	1.0	1.0

ᵃUnemployment Index = $\dfrac{\text{SMSA Unemployment Rate}}{\text{State Unemployment Rate}}$

ᵇMonth in which one bond issue was approved.

ᶜMonth in which two bond issues were approved.

Source: *Massachusetts Trends* Massachusetts Division of Employment Security.

trade-off between growth potential and ability to solve immediate unemployment problems. The high-growth industries tend to be high-wage, high-skill industries, and therefore they do not represent increased demand for unemployed low-skilled workers. Such industries remove local unemployment indirectly and inefficiently. On the other hand, those industries that do hire low-skilled workers tend to be declining industries and therefore may, in the long run, aggravate area unemployment problems. This dilemma may be specific to manufacturing. Unfortunately, industrial incentive programs have, up to this point, concentrated on manufacturing firms, perhaps reflecting the old saw that manufacturing is the key component in an area's export base. Expanded use of incentive programs within service industries would make sense. The service sector in recent years has been a high-growth sector, and the trend is expected to continue. In addition, possibilities for low-skilled jobs exist. But because the service industry is labor intensive, a capital subsidy program would be less attractive.

With respect to geographic areas, the Massachusetts experience indicates that those areas that need help the most participate very little in efforts to attract industry. Perhaps in regions with the most severe unemployment problems, a capital subsidy type of industrial incentive may not be the solution. Given the cost differentials involved in such locations, alternative programs may be required that either offer more attractive subsidies or attack area unemployment in a different manner, for example, training or out-migration programs.

Finally it is necessary for public policy makers to define the purpose of industrial incentive programs and to design and implement the programs according to that purpose. It appears that such is not the case. The Massachusetts program, for example, is intended to solve local unemployment problems, but the current law ties the bonds only loosely to area unemployment. If inducement programs are not intended to reduce unemployment by increasing local demand for those unemployed, and if programs are not implemented with that purpose in mind, then such programs are likely to result simply in shifting jobs from place to place and unemployment problems from area to area.

6

Implications for State and Federal Policy

In this chapter we summarize the findings of previous chapters and indicate what we consider the important policy questions at both the state and federal levels of government. We begin by pulling together the theoretical and empirical evidence concerning the effectiveness of state financial incentive programs, from the point of view of the state.

Program Cost to the State

The first issue of concern to the state is the cost of a financial incentive program. Chapter 3 examined this question in detail. Here we summarize that discussion and rank program alternatives, beginning with the least costly, that is, the program that generates the lowest cost to the incentive-granting state per dollar of subsidy to a participating firm.

Revenue bonds head the list. The only real costs to the state are administrative ones. The cost of the subsidy per se, which is an interest rate reduction, is borne by the federal government in income tax revenue foregone. Bondholders do not bear any costs (whether state residents or not) since the decision to purchase the tax-exempt bond is freely made and must compare favorably with alternative financial investments. There is the possibility, however, that revenue bond programs may serve to increase municipal bond rates in general.

A loan program financed by general obligation bonds, such as the New York State program, ranks second. If the state's borrowing rate is equal to its opportunity cost of funds, then the cost of the interest subsidy is again borne by the federal government. There are real costs to the state associated with administration of the program. In addition, there is the possibility of default costs. These, however, are likely to be insignificant; the state may be able to find another tenant to occupy the abandoned facilities. Finally, this type of program, if used heavily enough, could affect the state's bond rating and therefore its cost of borrowing.

A loan guarantee program can also be relatively costless to the state. We assume that the state issues general obligation bonds to finance an insurance fund. Participating firms are charged an interest premium by the state. If premium income is equal to defaults, there are no direct costs to the state other than administrative ones. If the state uses tax-exempt bonding to "bail out" a guaranteed firm, then the cost is again passed on to the federal government.

Lowest in rank of the interest subsidy programs is a Pennsylvania-style low-interest loan. As usual, there are administrative costs, and there is the possibility of default, although, as mentioned above, this may not result in significant costs to the state. Finally, there are real costs to the state associated with each loan since the interest charged by the state is less than its opportunity cost. Thus there is a net interest loss, which can be considerable, to the state. In Chapter 3 we estimated that the annual interest cost to Pennsylvania on one loan is as large as average annual administrative costs to the state.

Generally interest subsidy programs are attractive to states because they are relatively costless. The interest subsidy, except when the state lends at rates below its opportunity cost of funds, is borne by the federal government. However, any interest subsidy program will increase a firm's federal income tax liability since it results in lower interest expense deductions. Thus, to some extent, federal revenues are increased. The increased revenue in federal corporate income tax liability would, however, not be enough to offset the decreased revenue from the personal income tax liabilities of bondholders.

Tax subsidy programs rank last in terms of cost to the state. A tax exemption results in revenue losses to the state (or municipal government) equal in amount to the tax savings to the firm. They are therefore the most costly of the programs and, in this sense, the least desirable from the point of view of the state. However, a tax subsidy program will increase corporate income tax revenues to the federal government since state (local) tax deductions are reduced. Thus, unlike interest subsidy programs, tax subsidy programs result in a net increase in federal revenues. Whether state financial incentives represent a "raid on the Federal Treasury" depends then on whether interest subsidy or tax subsidy programs are used.

Impact on Location

The next major question of interest to the state is whether a financial incentive program can affect location decisions by firms and therefore have an impact on state investment, employment, and income. If other costs of production, marketing, and so on were constant over locations, the savings to the firm per dollar of project cost developed in Chapter 3 would give a measure of the effective construction and acquisition cost differentials that would be created by various programs. However, other costs do vary with location, so that the potential of state incentive programs to affect location is not that clear.

In Chapter 3 we estimated, for two-digit manufacturing industries, the maximum labor cost differential that various programs can potentially overcome. Depending on the nature of the subsidy and the capital intensity of the industry, financial incentive programs can overcome labor cost differentials of from less than 1 percent to 19 percent. The potential to alter location varies with the type of program, as described fully in Chapter 3, and increases with the capital intensity of the firm or industry.

Because of the large number of program-specific and firm-specific parameters that affect the cost savings potential of incentive programs, it is difficult to reach a conclusion a priori. Without empirical evidence one cannot reject the hypothesis that state financial incentives cannot affect location decisions.

In Chapter 4 we empirically estimated the impact that three prototype incentive programs had on state manufacturing investment activity. The three programs examined were the Connecticut loan guarantee program, the Pennsylvania loan program, and the Kentucky revenue bond program. Tax exemption schemes were not examined because they had been shown to be inefficient, relative to other forms of subsidy. Although each of the programs investigated was well established and well known, the empirical results of Chapter 4 remain somewhat specific to the states chosen for the study. The results are most easily generalized to other states within the same region that would have similar location cost differentials. With this in mind, we concluded in Chapter 4 that industrial revenue bonds are effective in inducing investment. A loan guarantee program, however, while also relatively costless to the state, is not beneficial; it does not serve to attract *additional* investment. Finally, a low-interest loan program appears to be effective. While there is some evidence to the contrary, the majority of the findings support its effectiveness.

Cost-Benefit to the State

The information on the cost of incentive programs to the state must then be compared with the gains to the state based on the empirical evidence concerning the impact of incentive programs on the location of industrial activity. A comparison of costs with gains, or benefits, provides a way of determining which programs are rational from the point of view of the state. A cost-benefit analysis of each of the three prototype programs was presented in Chapter 4. Both costs and benefits were measured in terms of income to the state.

Not surprisingly, the Kentucky revenue bond program has the highest ratio of benefits to costs. Our results suggest that one bond issue alone of less than $100,000 would create benefits to the state in excess of costs. Revenue bond programs are the least costly of the incentive programs to implement and have been shown, based on our Kentucky evidence, to be effective in luring industry.

The Pennsylvania loan program also has benefits well in excess of costs. Although the program is the most expensive of the interest subsidy programs, its positive impact on investment, as we estimated it, makes the program worthwhile to the state. The Connecticut loan guarantee program generates the opposite results. Although it is relatively costless, we found no evidence of any impact on state investment and therefore conclude that the costs, while small, exceed the benefits to the state.

Microeconomic Analysis: Policy Questions

Our microeconomic analysis was confined to the Massachusetts revenue bond program. We chose a revenue bond program because it ranked first in the cost-benefit analysis. We then chose Massachusetts because of the relative availability of data and because the state offered an exaggerated example of the kind of development problem that many of the other older industrial states also face.

In our microeconomic analysis we assumed that the bond program is effective in luring investment. The issue of concern was what kinds of industries participate in the incentive program and where these firms locate within the state. The real concern, then, is whether a program that increases state investment and income will solve area unemployment and growth problems within the state. While our analysis was confined to one program in one state, the results are likely to be similar for other programs used elsewhere, if program recipients are not restricted. This is because each of the efficient programs is a capital subsidy program of one kind or another and will therefore result in the same kind of trade-off problem that we found in Massachusetts. Here we repeat our conclusions from Chapter 5.

First, with respect to the kinds of industries that respond to an incentive program, there appears to be a trade-off between growth potential and ability to solve immediate unemployment problems. The high-growth industries tend to be high-wage, high-skill industries and therefore do not represent increased demand for unemployed low-skilled workers. Such industries remove local unemployment indirectly and inefficiently. On the other hand, those industries that hire those with lower skills tend to be declining industries and therefore may, in the long run, aggravate area unemployment problems. This dilemma may be specific to manufacturing. Unfortunately, industrial incentive programs have, up to this point, concentrated on manufacturing firms, perhaps reflecting the old saw that manufacturing is the key component in an area's export base. Expanded use of incentive programs within service industries would make sense. The service sector in recent years has been a high-growth sector, and the trend is expected to continue. In addition, possibilities for low-skilled jobs exist. But because the service industry is labor intensive, a capital subsidy program would be less attractive.

With respect to geographic areas, the Massachusetts experience indicates that those areas that need help the most participate very little in efforts to attract industry. Perhaps in regions with the most severe unemployment problems, a capital subsidy type of industrial incentive is not the solution. Given the cost differentials involved with such locations, alternative programs may be required that either offer more attractive subsidies or attack area unemployment in a different manner, for example, training or out-migration programs.

These findings generally weaken the argument in favor of state financial incentive programs if their purpose is to solve state unemployment problems. While some financial incentive programs appear to be capable of increasing state investment and income, they may neither decrease state unemployment rates nor tend to equalize growth rates within the state. What is required is that state public policy makers define the purpose of industrial incentive programs and design and implement the programs according to that purpose. If, for example, the purpose is to decrease unemployment, the amount of the subsidy can be tied to area unemployment (as in Pennsylvania), or subsidies can be restricted to firms that will increase local demand for those workers who are unemployed. The important thing is that policy makers recognize the limitations of financial incentive schemes in fulfilling what may be inconsistent objectives.

Regional and National Considerations

In this final section we change the perspective from that of the state to that of the region and nation as a whole. Up to this point we have argued that it may be rational for a state to introduce a financial incentive program; the state stands to gain more than it loses in terms of income, depending, of course, on the type of program. Our evidence suggests, however, that such gains may be enjoyed at the expense of neighboring states that either have no programs or have less effective ones. From the point of view of the region, then, there may be no net gain, and in fact there may be net losses to the extent that industry is diverted from least-cost locations, and resources are therefore misallocated.

This is not necessarily the case, however. Some argue that there can be net benefits to a region, as well as to the nation, if incentive programs fill a "credit gap." If the programs serve to supply funds to firms, which permit the participants to divert resources from other firms that would have made less productive use of them, then the programs produce net regional (national) benefits. The question is whether there is a credit gap, and if there is, whether the programs subsidize those firms experiencing credit difficulty. Our analysis of the Connecticut loan guarantee program suggested that such a diversion of resources did occur.[1] However, whether the program participants made better use of the resources remains a question. In Massachusetts, where we examined a revenue bond program, we found that all of the recipients were well-established firms and that a requirement for participation, in order to facilitate sale of the bond issue, was a respectable financial record.[2] This would seem to limit the applicability of the credit gap argument.

The second way that incentive programs can result in net regional or national benefits is by helping to compensate for wage rate inflexibility in labor surplus areas. If unemployment cannot be removed by a reduction in the wage rate and if labor is less mobile than capital, then it is necessary to increase investment in the labor surplus area in order to increase the demand for labor and reduce unemployment. The difficulties involved in effectively using a capital subsidy to reduce area unemployment have already been discussed. In addition, there is some evidence that while a program may reduce state unemployment, it may aggravate the unemployment problem elsewhere. In order for there to be net gains, the areas with the most severe labor surplus problems must have the most attractive incentives. In our analysis of the Pennsylvania program, we found that Pennsylvania did gain in employment at New Jersey's expense, and this occurred even when unemployment rates were lower in Pennsylvania than in New Jersey.[3] Our analysis of the Massachusetts program, detailed in Chapter 5, suggests that, within a state, the areas with the most severe unemployment problems participate least in the incentive program. These pieces of evidence argue against the potential of industrial incentives to produce net benefits to a region.

If, from a regional or national viewpoint, there are no net benefits from state financial incentive programs, what policy options are available? The easiest is to permit the programs to run their course, arguing that eventually, via laissez-faire, the programs will be neutralized. Each state, acting in self-defense, will enact similar programs so that, in the end, there will be no impact on locational choice. The only impact would be a reduction in federal revenues and a shifting of capital from nonsubsidized sectors into manufacturing. The problem is that the adjustment process is apparently very slow, so that in the interim there is the possibility for substantial resource misallocation.

The second possibility is for states to negotiate interstate agreements within regions to coordinate industrial inducement policies. States would have to cooperate on a regional level in order to guarantee net regional gains—or at least no regional losses. Most likely this approach would result in states within a region adopting similar programs so that, regionally, programs would be neutralized. To the extent that industrial location decisions are region specific, this would serve to neutralize programs in general and would therefore simply speed up the first outcome.

The last possibility is that Congress could make such programs illegal. There is, of course, reason for Congress to intervene if some states benefit at the expense of others. Since the federal government bears the cost, at least in part, of interest subsidy incentive programs, it could be argued that federal policy aggravates some states' unemployment problems and contributes to the misallocation of resources around the nation as a whole. The federal government could make amends by forbidding such programs. It is extremely unlikely, however, that state financial incentive programs can be eliminated very quickly. They enjoy a long history in the United States, and if anything, states appear to be becoming more creative in their efforts to act as financial intermediaries.[4] The best to hope for is that states recognize their regional interdependence and begin to coordinate their efforts to combat unemployment and promote industrial growth in the best interests of the region.

Appendixes

**Appendix A
Catalog of State Incentive
Programs**

Region and State	Bond Program	Loan Program	Mortgage Insurance Program	Tax Concession	Comments
New England					
Connecticut	Revenue	Yes	Yes	No	Revenue bonds issued by state.
Maine	Revenue	Yes	Yes	No	Revenue bonds issued by local authorities and must be approved by state.
Massachusetts	Revenue and general obligation	No	No	Yes	Bonds issued by local authorities. Credit against excise tax available
New Hampshire	No	Yes	Yes	No	Revenue bonds issued to finance loans and loan guarantees.
Rhode Island	Revenue	No	Yes	Yes	Revenue bonds issued by local authorities. Municipalities may grant property tax exemptions up to ten years or grant tax rate freezes.
Vermont	Revenue	No	Yes	Yes	Revenue bonds issued by local authorities. Projects financed by bonds are exempt from state and local taxes. Municipalities may freeze assessments or tax rates or grant property tax exemptions up to ten years.
Mid-Atlantic					
New Jersey	No	Yes	No	No	Loans can be made in only certain designated areas.
New York	Revenue	Yes	No	Yes	Revenue bonds issued by local authorities. Bond-financed projects may be exempted from property taxes. An income tax credit based on value of property or wage and salary bill is available to firms locating in certain urban or rural low-income areas. A 1 percent investment tax credit is available to other firms.

State	Type				Description
Pennsylvania	Revenue	Yes	No	No	Revenue bonds issued by local authorities. They may also issue tax-exempt mortgages, private placements subject to revenue bond restrictions.
East North Central					
Illinois	Revenue	Yes	No	No	Revenue bonds issued by local authorities.
Indiana	Revenue	Yes	Yes	No	Revenue bonds issued by local authorities.
Michigan	Revenue	No	No	Yes	Revenue bonds issued by local authorities. Cities may elect to exempt industrial projects in urban redevelopment areas from state, county, city, and special-district taxes for up to ten years.
Ohio	Revenue	No	Yes	No	Revenue bonds issued by both local and state authorities.
Wisconsin	Revenue	No	No	No	Revenue bonds issued by local authorities.
West North Central					
Iowa	Revenue	No	No	No	Revenue bonds issued by local authorities.
Kansas	Revenue	No	No	Yes	Revenue bonds issued by cities, which also have the option of exempting bond-financed projects from taxes for ten years.
Minnesota	Revenue	No	No	No	Revenue bonds issued by local authorities.
Missouri	Revenue and general obligation	No	No	No	Bonds issued by local authorities. General obligation bonds may be issued only in counties with 400,000 population or less.
Nebraska	Revenue	No	No	No	Revenue bonds issued by local authorities.
North Dakota	Revenue and general obligation	No	Yes	Yes	Bonds issued by local authorities with the exception that the state may issue bonds to finance construction of utilities. Recipients of local bond issues may receive a five-year exemption from local property and state income taxes.

Region and State	Bond Program	Loan Program	Mortgage Insurance Program	Tax Concession	Comments
North Dakota (cont.)					Other newly locating firms may negotiate partial or complete exemption from property taxes for five years. Alternatively, these firms may receive a tax credit of 1 percent of annual gross expenditure on state wages and salaries for three years, reduced to one-half of 1 percent in the fourth and fifth year.
South Dakota	Revenue	No	No	Yes	Revenue bonds issued by local authorities. Property tax exemption for a two-year period is available.
South Atlantic					
Delaware	Revenue and general obligation	No	No	No	The state issues both revenue and general obligation bonds and may guarantee repayment of local revenue bond issues.
Florida	Revenue	No	No	No	Revenue bonds issued by local authorities.
Georgia	Revenue	Yes	No	Yes	Revenue bonds issued by local authorities. Resulting projects are exempt from property taxation but usually make in-lieu payments. Purchases of manufacturing machinery for a new plant are exempt from the state sales tax.
Maryland	Revenue and general obligation	No	Yes	Yes	Bonds issued by local authorities. General obligation bonds may be issued by counties with high unemployment. Machinery and equipment are exempt from state property tax. Local governments may elect this exemption also (some exempt real property as well); period of exemption varies.
North Carolina	Revenue	No	No	No	Revenue bonds issued by local authorities.

State	Bond type				Notes
South Carolina	Revenue	No	No	Yes	Revenue bonds issued by local authorities but require state approval. Counties may exempt industrial projects from all county taxes except school taxes.
Virginia	Revenue	No	No	No	Revenue bonds issued by local authorities.
West Virginia	Revenue	Yes	No	Yes	Revenue bonds issued by local authorities. Projects financed by bonds are generally exempt from property taxation. A credit of 10 percent of the cost of investment in real or personal property against the gross sales is available to new or expanding firms.
East South Central					
Alabama	Revenue and general obligation	Yes	No	Yes	Bonds issued by local authorities. Projects financed by bonds are exempt from property taxation. New or expanding plants may be exempted from all state and local ad valorem taxes (except local school and land taxes) for ten years.
Kentucky	Revenue and general obligation	Yes	No	Yes	Bonds issued by local authorities. Projects financed by bonds are exempt from property taxation. Cities may exempt new establishments from city taxes for up to five years.
Mississippi	Revenue and general obligation	No	Yes	Yes	Bonds issued by local authorities. Projects financed by general obligation bonds are exempt from property taxation. New and expanding industries may be exempted from local taxes for ten years.
Tennessee	Revenue and general obligation	No	No	No	Bonds issued by local authorities. Projects financed by bonds are exempt from state and local taxes.

Region and State	Bond Program	Loan Program	Mortgage Insurance Program	Tax Concession	Comments
West South Central					
Arkansas	Revenue and general obligation	No	No	Yes	Bonds issued by local authorities. Revenue bond payments may be guaranteed by state. Investment in textile plants is exempt from local intangible property tax for seven years.
Louisiana	Revenue and general obligation	No	No	Yes	Bonds issued by local authorities. Bonds issued by municipalities (as opposed to public corporations) are not subject to state and local taxes. New and expanding industries may receive two consecutive five-year exemptions from property taxes; taxes on land and inventories not included.
Oklahoma	Revenue and general obligation	Yes	No	Yes	Bonds issued by local authorities. A five-year property tax exemption for industrial properties may be granted; exemption does not include land, school, and county taxes.
Texas	Revenue	Yes	No	No	Revenue bonds issued by local authorities. Loan program finances new industry in rural areas only.
Mountain					
Arizona	Revenue	No	No	No	Revenue bonds issued by local authorities.
Colorado	Revenue	No	No	No	Revenue bonds issued by local authorities.
Idaho	No	No	No	No	
Montana	Revenue	No	No	Yes	Revenue bonds issued by local authorities. New industrial property is taxed at 7 percent of assessed value for first three years of operation.

Nevada	No	No	No	Revenue	Revenue bonds issued by local authorities.
New Mexico	No	No	No	Revenue	Revenue bonds issued by local authorities; they may be also used to cover moving costs and to provide operating capital. Bond-financed projects are exempt from all state and local taxes.
Utah	No	No	No	Revenue	Revenue bonds issued by local authorities. Bond-financed projects are exempt from all state and local taxes.
Wyoming	No	No	No	Revenue	Revenue bonds issued by local authorities.
Pacific					
Alaska	Yes	No	No	Revenue	Revenue bonds issued by state.
California	No	Yes	No	No	
Hawaii	Yes	Yes	Yes	Revenue and general obligation	Bonds issued by local authorities. Revenue bond-financed projects are exempt from state and local taxes. A new business may be granted a five-year exemption from state and local taxes.
Oregon	No	No	No	Revenue	Revenue bond authorization limited to port districts.
Washington	Yes	No	No	Revenue and general obligation	Bond authorization limited to port districts. Loan program provides funds only for improvements to industrial sites.

Sources: New York State Department of Commerce, *The Use of Public Funds or Credit in Industrial Location* (Albany, January 1974); Laurence H. Falk and Gregory H. Wassall, *Inducement Programs in the New Jersey Area* (New Brunswick, New Jersey: Rutgers Bureau of Economic Research, 1972).

Appendix B
Estimates of the
Composition of
Manufacturing Facility
Costs

In this appendix the composition of expenditures on land, plant, and machinery, and equipment in a typical manufacturing facility is estimated. The procedure can be explained in the following two steps.

1. Expenditures on plant versus machinery and equipment. For the years in which incentive programs were operative, the proportions of capital expenditures that the categories above constituted can be obtained from data in various issues of the U.S. Department of Commerce, *Annual Survey* and *Census of Manufactures* (Washington, D.C.: U.S. Government Printing Office). From this we find that spending on plant averaged 28 percent and on machinery and equipment 72 percent throughout the period.

Since machinery and equipment turn over more rapidly than plant, the above data must be adjusted to reflect average proportions in a new facility. In the early 1960s, the average life of machinery and equipment was thirteen years, of plant, twenty-three years.[a] Thus machinery and equipment turn over 1.77 times during the life of a plant. A new factory, therefore, can be estimated to include capital expenditures consisting of 41 percent plant and 59 percent machinery and equipment.

2. Estimation of expenditures on land. No good source of data was found. Conversations with industrial realtors and industrial development specialists led to the conclusion that land typically constitutes 10 percent of total project costs. This was borne out by limited empirical evidence.

Combining our information leads to an estimate of a new industrial facility typically consisting of, in terms of cost, 53 percent machinery and equipment, 37 percent plant, and 10 percent land. In some examples, these estimates were rounded to 50, 40, and 10 percent, respectively. Obviously, these figures will vary considerably for individual plants.

[a] See Robert E. Hall and Dale W. Jorgensen, "Application of the Theory of Optimal Capital Accumulation," in *Tax Incentives and Capital Spending*, ed. Gary Fromm (Washington, D.C.: The Brookings Institution, 1971), p. 31.

Notes

Notes

Chapter 2
The History and Practice of Statewide Industrial Incentives

1. Goodbody and Company, *Industrial Aid Financing* (New York, 1965), p. 4.

2. Ibid., p. 2.

3. In 1960, 72 percent of all IDB issues in the country were of the general obligation type; the corresponding percentage in Mississippi was 100 percent. In 1967, 11 percent were general obligation bonds countrywide; in Mississippi, the figure was 86 percent. Edwin C. Gooding, "The New Status Of Industrial Aid Bonds," *New England Business Review*, November 1968, pp. 3-4.

4. The last figure is derived from New York State Department of Commerce, *The Use of Public Funds or Credit in Industrial Location* (Albany, January 1974), pp. 8-92. All forty-six of these states permitted revenue bond financing; thirteen also allowed the use of general obligation bonds for industrial development. This amount does not correspond to the publication's own tally because it classifies state-administered bond programs as loan programs; here they are classified as bond programs. Data for earlier years are from William Edward Morgan, "The Effects of State and Local Tax and Financial Inducements on Industrial Location" (Ph.D. diss., University of Colorado, 1964), p. 118.

5. These figures are Investment Bankers' Association-Securities Industry of America estimates, which are believed to be subject to serious underreporting. For further discussion and some other estimates, see Table 2-1.

6. However, municipal decisions to attract particular firms via bond financing had to be approved by a state board. Because of the stringency adopted by this board in screening applicants, relatively little financing was actually consummated under the BAWI program. For further discussion, see John E. Moes, *Local Subsidies for Industry* (Chapel Hill: University of North Carolina Press, 1962), pp. 76-80.

7. Alabama Business Research Council, *Industrial Development Financing: Business and Community Experience and Opinions* (1970), p. 10, and New York State Department of Commerce, *Use of Public Funds*, pp. 4-6. Of these forty-three states, fourteen provide financing through a local nonprofit agency, and thirty-five permit the municipal or county government to provide financing directly. Six states maintain both financing plans.

8. Ibid., p. 19.

9. Moes, *Local Subsidies for Industry*. He synthesizes his arguments in "The Subsidization of Industry by Local Communities in the South," *Southern Economic Journal* 28 (1961): 187-93.

10. See Irving J. Goffman, "Local Subsidies for Industry: Comment," *Southern Economic Journal* 29 (1962): 111-14; James H. Thompson "Local Subsidies for Industry: Comment," *Southern Economic Journal* 29 (1962): 114-19; John H. Cumberland and Fritz Von Beck, "Regional Economic Development Objectives and Subsidization of Local Industry," *Land Economics* 43 (1967): 253-64.

11. *Albritten v. City of Winoma*, 303 U.S. 624, 82 L. Ed., 1088 (1938).

12. Rev. Rul. 54-106, Cum. Bull. 1954-1, p. 28.

13. Rev. Rul. 57-187, Cum. Bull. 1957-1, p. 65.

14. Rev. Rul. 63-20, Cum. Bull. 1963-1, p. 24.

15. Section 107 of the Revenue and Expenditure Control Act of 1968, passed in June by the second session of the 90th Congress.

16. Public Law 90-634, *Laws of the 90th Congress—2nd Session*. More generally, this law distinguishes between an "industrial development bond" and other types of exempt municipal securities. An IDB is defined in section 103(C) (1) as an obligation

(A) which is issued as part of an issue all or a major portion of which are to be used directly or indirectly in any trade or business carried on by any person who is not an exempt person . . . and
(B) the payment of the principal or interest on which (under the terms of such obligation or any underlying arrangement) is, in whole or major part—
    (i) secured by any interest in property used or to be used in a trade or business or in payments in respect of such property, or
    (ii) to be derived from payments in respect of property, or borrowed money, used or to be used in a trade or business.

Thus, IDBs are taxable. Exemptions are then listed and include bonds for residential housing for family units, sports facilities, convention or trade show facilities, sewage and solid waste disposal facilities, facilities for the local furnishing of electric energy or gas, air and water pollution control facilities, and water facilities. Refunding issues for issues prior to January 1, 1969, are also exempt. And, finally, any IDB issue under the $1 million-5 million limitation is exempt. See William G. McCollom, "Industrial Development Bonds and Tax Policy: A Trend Toward Vivisection of Public Finance," *The Tax Lawyer* 23 (1970): 383-97, and C. Willis Ritter, "Federal Income Tax Treatment of Municipal Obligations: Industrial Development Bonds," *The Tax Lawyer* 25 (1972): 511-36.

17. Unless otherwise noted, such comparative figures are drawn from New York State Department of Commerce, *Use of Public Funds*. For information about specific states, see Appendix A to this book.

18. For example, in the Northeast, one out of six states surveyed with revenue bond enabling legislation specifically provided for tenant ownership. See Laurence H. Falk and Gregory H. Wassall, *Inducement Programs in the New Jersey Area* (New Brunswick: Rutgers Bureau of Economic Research, 1972), pp. 13-26.

19. David H. Nelson, "Tax Considerations of Municipal Industrial Incentive Financing," *Taxes—The Tax Magazine* 45 (1967): 946.

20. Ibid., p. 945.

21. Benjamin Bridges, Jr., "State and Local Inducements for Industry, Part I," *National Tax Journal* 18 (1965): 2-6, and New York State Department of Commerce, *Use of Public Funds*, pp. 8-92. For more information about specific states, see Appendix A to this book.

22. Edwin C. Gooding, "New War Between the States," *New England Business Review*, October 1963, p. 1. The South's "weapons" are bond financing and tax exemptions.

23. Edwin C. Gooding, "New War Between the States, Part II," *New England Business Review*, December 1963, p. 2.

24. Joseph Dorfman, *The Economic Mind in American Civilization, 1606-1865* (London: George G. Harrap and Company, 1947), pp. 291-92. Also, local government debt was used to finance the firm.

25. Morgan, "Effects of State and Local Tax," p. 116.

26. Moes, *Local Subsidies to Industry*, pp. 85-86, and Bridges, "Inducements for Industry," p. 3.

27. Morgan, "Effects of State and Local Tax," pp. 124-34. The states are Alabama, Kentucky, Louisiana, Mississippi, Rhode Island, South Carolina, and Vermont. Many of the exemptions were in conjunction with bond issues.

28. Two examples of this bifurcated motive to eliminate business personalty taxes are quoted below. First from Governor William L. Guy, "1965 Message to the North Dakota Legislature," p. 11: "After decades of effort, we must admit that fair administration of the personal property tax is beyond possibility. . . . It discourages investment in productive tools and is a depressant on our economy."

The second is from Connecticut, *The Report of the Governor's Commission on Tax Reform* (Hartford, December 18, 1972), 2: 24: "*The Commission concluded that the personal property tax is extremely difficult to administer equitably*. The tax is a major deterrant to business and industrial investment in the State."

29. Twenty-three states exempt pollution control facilities from real and/or personal property taxes. National Tax Association Property Tax Committee, "The Erosion of the Ad Valorem Real Estate Tax Base," *Tax Policy* 40 (1973): 29.

30. Ibid., p. 50.

31. Advisory Commission on Intergovernmental Relations, *State-Local Taxation and Industrial Location* (Washington, D.C., 1967), p. 49.

32. Ibid., p. 50.

33. See William J. Stober and Laurence H. Falk, "Poorly Conceived Financial Inducements: A Study of Louisiana's Gas Severance Tax Rebate," *Social Science Quarterly* 51 (1970): 108-19.

Chapter 3
The Value of Financial Incentives to the Firm: A Model

1. An earlier version of this model was developed by William J. Stober and Laurence H. Falk and applied to estimating "efficiency

ratios'' for revenue bonds and property tax exemptions. See ''Property Tax Exemption: An Inefficient Subsidy to Industry,'' *National Tax Journal* 20 (1967): 386-94; ''Industrial Development Bonds as a Subsidy to Industry,'' *National Tax Journal* 22 (1969): 232-43; ''The Effect of Financial Inducements on the Location of Firms,'' *Southern Economic Journal* 36 (1969): 25-35.

2. See Sidney Davisdon and David F. Drake, ''Capital Budgeting and the 'Best' Tax Depreciation Method,'' *Journal of Business* 34 (1961): 442-52.

3. For further discussion, see William Edward Morgan, ''The Effects of State and Local Tax and Financial Inducements on Industrial Location'' (Ph.D. diss., University of Colorado, 1964), pp. 124-34.

4. See U.S., Bureau of the Census, Census of Governments, *Taxable Property Values and Assessment-Sales Price Ratios and Tax Rates* (Washington, D.C.: U.S. Government Printing Office, 1973, 1968), vol. 2.

5. For example, Oliver Oldman and Henry Aaron, ''Assessment-Sales Ratios Under the Boston Property Tax,'' *National Real Tax Journal* 18 (1965): 36-49; Theodore Reynolds Smith, Property Taxation and the Urban Center (Hartford: John C. Lincoln Institute, 1972), esp. ch. 7.

6. See Advisory Commission on Intergovernmental Relations, *The Property Tax—Reform and Relief* (Washington, D.C., November 1973), p. 509; U.S., Congress, Senate, Subcommittee on Intergovernmental Relations of the Committee on Government Operations, *Status of Property Tax Administration in the States*, 93d Cong., 1st sess., March 23, 1973. The latter study lists eight states with classification systems, of which six are legally empowered to grant exemptions.

7. Data were obtained from National Tax Association Property Tax Committee, ''The Erosion of the Ad Valorem Real Estate Tax Base,'' *Tax Policy* 40 (1973): Appendix A, 50-68.

8. For data on asset lifetimes used in the Class Life Asset Depreciation Range System, see *1974 U.S. Master Tax Guide* (Chicago: Commerce Clearing House, 1973), pp. 412-31.

9. For a more comprehensive discussion of leasing versus owning industrial property, see William N. Kinnard, Jr., and Stephen D.

Messner, *Industrial Real Estate* (Washington, D.C.: Society of Industrial Realtors, 1973), pp. 324-28.

10. Gerald W. Sazama, "State Government Industrial Loan Programs" (Ph.D. diss., University of Wisconsin, 1967), p. 160.

11. Stober and Falk, "Effect of Financial Inducements," p. 34.

Chapter 4
Macroeconomic Estimates of Program Effectiveness

1. See Gerald W. Sazama, "State Government Industrial Loan Programs" (Ph.D. diss., University of Wisconsin, 1967), pp. 93-165; Ronald B. Gold, "Subsidies to Industry in Pennsylvania," *National Tax Journal* 19 (1966): 286-97.

2. For a detailed discussion of questionnaire studies, see Benjamin Bridges, Jr., *State and Local Industrial Development Incentives: Wisconsin, Its Neighbor States, and the Nation* (Madison: Wisconsin: Department of Resource Development, 1965), ch. 5.

3. For a discussion and examples of comparative cost studies, see Walter Isard, *Methods of Regional Analysis: An Introduction to Region Science* (Cambridge: MIT Press, 1960), ch. 7.

4. William J. Stober and Laurence H. Falk, "Industrial Development Bonds as a Subsidy to Industry," *National Tax Journal* 22 (1969): 232-43, and "The Effect of Financial Inducements on the Location of Firms," *Southern Economic Journal* 36 (1969): 25-35; Benjamin Bridges, Jr., "State and Local Inducements for Industry, Part II," *National Tax Journal* 18 (1965): 175-92; and Gold, "Subsidies to Industry."

5. For a review and bibliography, see Dale W. Jorgenson, "Econometric Studies of Investment Behavior: A Survey," *Journal of Economic Literature* 9 (1971): 1111-47.

6. Ibid., 1111-13.

7. For all three states, investment and value added data were obtained from U.S. Bureau of the Census, *Annual Survey* and *Census of Manufactures*, various issues. The data were then deflated by the appropriate GNP price deflators. Interest rates for high grade industrial bonds were obtained from U.S. Department of Commerce, *Survey of Current Business*, various issues. Data on amounts lent in the programs were obtained directly from state authorities.

8. For an excellent review of cost-benefit procedure, see A. R.

Prest and R. Turvey, "Cost-Benefit Analysis: A Survey," *The Economic Journal* 75 (1965): 683-735.

9. Sazama, "State Government Industrial Loan Programs," p. 160.

10. Gold, "Subsidies to Industry," p. 292.

Chapter 5
Microeconomic Analysis of Program Efficiency

1. K.J. Crepas and R.A. Stevenson, "Industrial Aid Bonds: Too Capital Intensive?" *Commercial and Financial Chronicle* 208, no. 6810 (August 1968).

2. Another potential source of net aggregate benefits is if the program fills a "credit gap." See Benjamin Bridges, Jr., "State and Local Inducements for Industry, Part II," *National Tax Journal* 9 (June 1956).

3. There is a state tax incentive scheme tied to provision of training to low-skilled, unemployed individuals, the Urban Job Incentive Program. Although in existence since 1970, it has not been a very active program. For details, see D. Hellman, "A Survey of Industrial Inducement Efforts and Their Application in Massachusetts," Massachusetts Public Finance Project Report No. 28 (Lynn, Massachusetts, 1974).

4. U.S. Department of Commerce, Bureau of the Census, *Statistical Abstract of the United States: 1975* (Washington, D.C.: Government Printing Office, 1975), p. 364.

5. U.S. Department of Labor, Bureau of Labor Statistics, *Employment and Earnings* 21, no. 7 (January 1975).

6. Ibid.

Chapter 6
Implications for State and Federal Policy

1. For details see Daryl Hellman, L.H. Falk, and Gregory C. Wassall, "Loan Guarantees as Location Incentives: An Empirical Evaluation of the Connecticut Program," *Atlantic Economic Journal* 3 (1975): 53-60.

2. See Daryl Hellman, Gregory H. Wassall, and Herb Es-

kowitz, "The Role of Statewide Industrial Incentive Programs in the New England Economy," *The New England Journal of Business & Economics* 1 (1975): 10-29.

3. Laurence H. Falk, Daryl Hellman, Peter D. Loeb, and Gregory H. Wassall, "The Effect of the Pennsylvania Industrial Loan Program on Employment in New Jersey," paper presented at the Southern Regional Science Association Meetings, Atlanta, Georgia, April 1975.

4. See Ralph C. Kimball, "States as Financial Intermediaries," *New England Economic Review* (1976): 17-29.

Bibliography

Advisory Commission on Intergovernmental Relations, *Industrial Development Bond Financing*. Washington, D.C., 1963.

_____. *The Property Tax—Reform and Relief*. Washington, D.C., 1973.

_____. *State-Local Taxation and Industrial Location*. Washington, D.C., 1973.

Alabama Business Research Council. *Industrial Development Bond Financing: Business and Community Experiences and Opinions*. Alabama, 1970.

Apilado, Vincent P. "Financial Incentives, Industrial Development and Economic Growth." *Local Finance* 3 (1974): 3-17.

Arizona Development Board. *Tax Comparisons Between the States of Arizona and California of Specific Mythical Corporations*. Phoenix, 1964.

Arrow, Kenneth J. "Discounting and the Public Investment Criteria." In *Water Research*, edited by Allen V. Kneese and Stephen C. Smith. Baltimore: The Johns Hopkins Press, 1966.

Baumol, William J. *Business Behavior, Value and Growth*. Rev. ed. New York: Harcourt, Brace & World, 1967.

_____. "On the Social Rate of Discount," *American Economic Journal* 58 (1968): 788-802.

Beaton, Charles R., and Young P. Joun. *The Effect of the Property Tax on Manufacturing Location*. Fullerton, California: California State College, 1968.

Beckmann, Martin. *Location Theory*. New York: Random House, 1968.

Bergin, Thomas P., and William F. Eagen. "Economic Growth and Community Facilities." *Municipal Finance* 33 (1961): 146-55.

Bethune Jones. "Industrial Promotion Trends in the States." *From the State Capitols*. Periodically published reports, 1970 to date.

"A Better Way to Finance a New Plant Site"' *Business Management* 30 (1966): 41-46.

Bischoff, Charles W. "The Effect of Alternative Lag Distributions." In *Tax Incentives and Capital Spending*, edited by Gary Fromm. Washington, D.C.: The Brookings Institution, 1971.

Black, J. "Investment Allowances, Initial Allowances and Cheap Loans as a Means of Encouraging Investment." *Review of Economic Studies* 27 (1959): 44-49.

Bonser, Charles F., et al. *Business Taxation in Indiana*. Indianapolis: Indiana Commission on State Tax and Financing Policy, 1966.

Borts, George H. "Criteria for the Evaluation of Regional Development Programs," In *Regional Accounts for Policy Decisions*, edited by Werner Z. Hirsch. Baltimore: The Johns Hopkins Press, 1966.

_____. "The Equalization of Returns and Regional Growth." *American Economic Review* 50 (1960): 319-47.

_____. "Growth and Capital Movements Among United States Regions in the Post War Period." In *Essays in Regional Economics*, edited by John F. Kain and John R. Meyer. Cambridge: Harvard University Press, 1971.

Bowlin, Oswald D. "Private Business and Industrial Aid Bonds." *Atlanta Economic Review* 13 (1963): 10-15.

Bradley, Joseph F., and Oswald D. Bowlin. "Industrial Aid Bonds—A Device for Attracting New Industry." *Municipal Finance* 33 (1961): 150-55.

Bratter, Herbert. "Should Tax-Free Industrial Revenue Bonds Be Eliminated?" *Banking* 59 (1966): 62.

Bridges, Benjamin, Jr. *Industrial Incentive Programs: Analysis of State and Local Industrial Development Incentives: Wisconsin, Its Neighbor States and the Nation*. Madison: Wisconsin Department of Resource Development, 1965.

_____. "State and Local Government Financial Inducements for Industry." In Tax Institute of America, *State and Local Taxes on Business. Symposium . . . October 1964*. Princeton, N.J., 1965.

_____. "State and Local Inducements for Industry, Part I." *National Tax Journal* 18 (1965): 1-14.

_____. "State and Local Inducements for Industry, Part II." *National Tax Journal* 18 (1965): 175-92.

Brown, E. Cary. "Tax Incentives for Investment." *American Economic Review Papers ad Proceedings* 53 (1962): 335-46.

Browne, Alan K. "Misuse of Public Credit to Aid Private Enterprise: The Case Against Municipal Industrial Revenue Bonds." In Tax Institute of America, *State and Local Taxes on Business. Symposium . . . October 1964*. Princeton, N.J., 1965.

Buchanan, James M., and John E. Moes. "A Regional Countermeasure to National Wage Standardization." *American Economic Review* 50 (1960): 434-38.

Buehler, Alfred G. *Tax Study—State of Connecticut*. Hartford, 1963.

Camil, William. *Attracting Industry into California Cities: Legal Inducements and Annexations*. Occasional Paper Series No. 3 Davis: Institute of Governmental Affairs, University of California, 1964.

Campbell, Alan K. *Effect of Industrial Location on Revenues and Expenditures of Municipalities*. Washington, D.C.: Municipal Finance Officers Association, 1961.

_____. "State and Local Taxes, Expenditures, and Economic Development." In Tax Institute of America, *State and Local Taxes on Business. Symposium . . . October 1964*. Princeton, N.J., 1965.

_____. "Taxes and Industrial Location in the New York Metropolitan Region." *National Tax Journal* 11 (1958): 195-218.

Chase, Sam B., Jr. "Tax Credits for Investment Spending." *National Tax Journal* 15 (1962): 32-52.

Cobleigh, Ira U. "The Virtues of Industrial Revenue Bonds." *Commercial and Financial Chronicle* (1967): 801.

Coen, Robert M. "Tax Policy and Investment Behavior: Comment." *American Economic Review* 59 (1969): 370-79.

Cohen, Jerome B., and Sidney M. Robbins. *The Financial Manager*. New York: Harper & Row, 1966.

"Companies Rush for Cheaper Money. Industrial Development Bonds Find New Popularity as Business Hunts Ways to Keep Financing Costs Down." *Business Week* (June 11, 1966): 114.

Connecticut. Public Act 484 (Connecticut Industrial Building Commission). Hartford, 1965.

_____. *The Report of the Governor's Commission on Tax Reform*. Vol. 2. Hartford, December 18, 1972.

Connecticut Industrial Building Commission. *Administrative Regulations Insuring of Industrial Mortgages*. Hartford, 1968.

————. *Application and Instruction for Mortgage Insurance on an Industrial Project Consisting of New Machinery and Equipment*. Hartford, 1964.

————. *Building a Greater Connecticut: 1971 Report of the Connecticut Industrial Building Commission*.

Connecticut Tax Study Commission. *Taxation of Business Personalty*. Hartford, 1967.

Cook, John W. "The Investment Credit—*Investment Incentive and Countercyclical Tool.*" *Taxes* 45:227-33.

Cragg, John G.; Arnold C. Hargerber; and Peter Mieszkowski. "Empirical Evidence on the Incidence of the Corporation Income Tax." *Journal of Political Economy* 75 (1967): 811-21.

Creamer, Daniel. *Capital Expansion and Capacity in Postwar Manufacturing*. New York: National Industrial Conference Board, 1961.

————. "Shifts of Manufacturing Industries." *Industrial Location and National Resources*. Washington, D.C.: U.S. National Resources Planning Board, 1942.

Crepas, Kenneth J., and Richard A. Stevenson. "Are Industrial Aid Bonds Fulfilling Their Intended Purpose?" *Financial Analysts Journal* 24 (1968): 105-108.

————. "Industrial Aid Bonds: Too Capital Intensive?" *Commercial and Financial Chronicle* 208 (1968): 528.

Cumberland, John H., and Frits van Beek. "Regional Economic Development Objectives and Subsidization of Local Industry." *Land Economics* 43 (1967): 253-64.

Davidson, Sidney, and David F. Drake. "Capital Budgeting and the 'Best' Tax Depreciation Method." *Journal of Business* 34 (1961): 442-52.

Delaware State Development Department. *Finance: Delaware Offers Financing for Creative Industry*. Dover, 1969.

————. *Taxes: Corporate Dollars Go Further in Delaware*. Dover, 1969.

DeVyver, Frank T. "Labor Factors and the Industrial Development of the South." *Southern Economic Journal* 18 (1951): 189-205.

Dorfman, Joseph. *The Economic Mind in American Civilization, 1606-1865*. London: George C. Harrap & Co., 1947.

Dorfman, Robert. "Basic Economic and Technological Concepts:

A General Statement." In *Design of Water Resource Systems*, edited by Arthur Maass et al. Cambridge: Harvard University Press, 1962.

Due, John F. "Studies of State-Local Tax Influences on Location of Industry." *National Tax Journal* 14 (1961): 163-73.

Dunn, Robert M., Jr. "A Problem of Bias in Benefit-Cost Analysis: Consumer Surplus Reconsidered." *The Southern Economic Journal* 33 (1967): 337-42.

Durand, David. "The Cost of Capital, Corporation Finance, and the Theory of Investment: Comment." *American Economic Review* 49 (1959): 639-55.

Eckstein, Otto. "A Survey of the Theory of Public Expenditure Criteria." *Public Finance: Needs, Sources and Utilization*. Princeton: Princeton University Press, 1961.

_____. *Water-Resource Development: The Economics of Project Evaluation*. Cambridge: Harvard University Press, 1958.

Eisner, Robert. "Tax Policy and Investment Behavior: Comment." *American Economic Review* 59 (1969): 379-88.

Falk, Laurence H.; Daryl Hellman; Peter D. Loeb; and Gregory H. Wassall. "The Effect of the Pennsylvania Industrial Loan Program on Employment in New Jersey." Paper presented at the Southern Regional Science Association Meeting, Atlanta, Georgia, April 3, 1975.

_____. *An Industrial Inducement Program for New Jersey: Empirical Findings and Recommendations*. New Brunswick: Rutgers Bureau of Economic Research, 1973.

Falk, Laurence H., and Alan C. Ringquist. "Industrial Inducements in the New Jersey Area: Preliminary Report, The Relative Efficiency of State Loan Programs for Industry." Rutgers Bureau of Economic Research. Unpublished report. 1971.

_____. "Industrial Inducements in the New Jersey Area: Preliminary Report No. 2. The Relative Efficiency of State Loan Programs for Industry." Rutgers Bureau of Economic Research. Unpublished report, 1971.

Falk, Laurence H., and William J. Stober. *An Economic Reappraisal of the Toledo Bend Multiple-Purpose Water Project*. Louisiana Water Resources Research Institute, Bulletin 7, Baton Rouge: Louisiana State University, 1970.

_____. *The Measurement and Comparison of Costs for Alternative*

Water Replacement Projects. Louisiana Water Resources Research Institute, Bulletin 2. Baton Rouge, 1966.

Falk, Laurence H., and Gregory H. Wassall. *Inducement Programs in the New Jersey Area*. New Brunswick: Rutgers Bureau of Economic Research, 1972.

Feldstein, Martin S. "Derivation of Social Time Preference Rates." *Kyklos* 18 (1965): 277-87.

————. "Net Social Benefit Calculation and the Public Investment Decision." *Oxford Economic Papers* 16 (1964): 114-31.

————. "Opportunity Cost Calculations in Benefit-Cost Analysis." *Public Finance* 2 (1964): 117-39.

Fernbach, Frank L. "Subsidized Plant Migration." *AFL-CIO American Federationist* 73 (1966): 8-12.

Fieschko, Theodore M. "State Tax Incentives." *Taxes—the Tax Magazine* 45 (1967): 222-26.

Fischel, William A. "Fiscal and Environmental Considerations in the Location of Firms in Suburban Communities." Ph.D. dissertation' Princeton University, 1974.

Fisher, Franklin M. "Discussion." In *Tax Incentives and Capital Spending*, edited by Gary Fromm. Washington, D.C.: The Brookings Institution, 1971.

Floyd, Charles F. "Financing Industrial Development: Municipal Industrial Development Bonds." *Georgia Business* 27 (1967): 1-5.

Floyd, Joe S., Jr. "Federal, State and Local Government Programs for Financing Industrial Development." In *Proceedings of the 55th Annual Conference on Taxation (1962)*, National Tax Association.

————. "State and Local Financing for Industrial Development." In *Proceedings of the 56th Annual Conference on Taxation (1963)*, National Tax Association.

————, and L. Hodges. *Financing Industrial Growth: Private and Public Sources of Long Term Capital for Industry*. Research Paper 10, School of Business Administration. Chapel Hill: University of North Carolina, 1962.

Fox, William F. "Property Tax Influences on Industrial Location within a Metropolitan Area." A Report for the Department of Economics and Community Development, State of Ohio, 1973.

Fromm, Gary, ed. *Tax Incentives and Capital Spending*. Washington, D.C.: The Brookings Institution, 1971.

Fuchs, Victor R. *Changes in the Location of Manufacturing in the United States Since 1929*. New Haven: Yale University Press, 1962.

Goffman, Irving J. "Local Subsidies for Industry: Comment." *Southern Economic Journal* 29 (1962): 111-14.

Gold, Ronald B. "Subsidies to Industry in Pennsylvania." *National Tax Journal* 19 (1966): 286-97.

Goodbody & Co. *Industrial Aid Financing*. New York, 1965.

Gooding, Edwin C. "The New Status of Industrial Aid Bonds— Implications for State and Local Financing Efforts." *New England Business Review*, November 1968, 2-9.

_____. "New War Between the States." *New England Business Review*, October 1964, 2-7.

_____. "Tax Structure, Tax Competition and Tax Burdens on Industry, Part 2." *New England Business Review*, February 1968, 2-10.

Gray, Ralph. "An Economic View of Municipal Subsidies to Industry." *Municipal Finance* 36 (1964): 153-60.

_____. "Industrial Development Subsidies and Efficiency in Resource Allocation." *National Tax Journal* 17 (1964): 164-72.

Greenhut, M.L. *Microeconomics and the Space Economy*. Chicago: Scott Foresman & Co., 1963.

_____. *Plant Location in Theory and in Practice*. Chapel Hill: University of North Carolina Press, 1956.

_____. *A Theory of the Firm in Economic Space*. New York: Appleton-Century-Crofts, 1970.

Grossfield, K. "The Effectiveness of Investment Incentives." *Banker* 119 (1969): 1028-37.

Groves, Harold M., and John Riew. "The Impact of Industry on Local Taxes—A Simple Model." *National Tax Journal* 17 (1963): 137-45.

Guy, William L., Governor. "1965 Message to the North Dakota Legislature." 1965.

Hale, Carl W. *The Contribution of Local Subsidies to the Economic Development of West Virginia, 1956-1966*. Economic Development Series No. 12, Bureau of Business Research, College of Commerce. Morgantown, West Virginia: West Virginia University, 1969.

———. "Local Subsidies: Regional Development or Regional Rivalry?" *American Industrial Development Council Journal* 3 (1968): 33-53.

———. "The Optimality of Local Subsidies in Regional Development Programs." *Quarterly Review of Economics and Business (1969):* 35-50.

Hall, Robert E., and Dale W. Jorgenson. "Application of the Theory of Optimum Capital Accumulation." In *Tax Incentives and Capital Spending*, edited by Gary Fromm. Washington, D.C.: The Brookings Institution, 1971.

———. "Tax Policy and Investment Behavior." *American Economic Review* 57 (1967): 391-414.

———. "Tax Policy and Investment Behavior: Reply and Further Results." *American Economic Review* 59 (1969): 388-401.

Hamer, Andrew W. "The Comparative Costs of Manufacturing Firms in Urban Areas: A Boston Case Study." *Review of Regional Studies* 2 (1972): 95-134.

Hammond, R.J. *Benefit Cost Analyses and Water Pollution Control*. Stanford: Stanford University, 1959.

Harberger, Arnold C. "Discussion." In *Tax Incentives and Capital Spending*, edited by Gary Fromm. Washington, D.C.: The Brookings Institution, 1971.

———. "The Incidence of the Corporation Income Tax." *Journal of Political Economy* 70 (1962): 215-40.

Harline, Osmond L. "How States Compete for New Industry." *Utah Economic and Business Review* 24 (1964): 1-9.

Harris, Chauncy D. "The Market as a Factor in the Localization of Industry in the United States." *Annals of the Association of American Geographers* 44 (1954): 315-47.

Hellman, Daryl. *A Survey of Industrial Inducement Efforts and Their Application to Massachusetts*. Lynn: Massachusetts Public Finance Project Report No. 28, June 1974.

———; L.H. Falk; and Gregory H. Wassall. "Loan Guarantees as Location Incentives: An Empirical Evaluation of Connecticut's Program." *Atlantic Economic Journal* 3 (1975): 53-60.

Hellman, Daryl, and Gregory H. Wassall. "The Effectiveness of Industrial Incentive Programs and Their Relevance to the New England Economy." Paper presented at the New England Business and Economic Development Conference, Portsmouth, New Hampshire, October 18, 1974.

Hellman, Daryl; Gregory H. Wassall; and Herb Eskowitz. "The Role of Statewide Industrial Incentive Programs in the New England Economy." *The New England Journal of Business and Economics* 1 (1975): 10-29.

Hildebrand, George H., and Arthur Mace, Jr. "The Employment Multiplier in an Expanding Industrial Market: Los Angeles County, 1940-47." *Review of Economics and Statistics* 32 (1950): 241-49.

Hildebrand, George H., and Ta Chung Liu. *Manufacturing Production Functions in the United States*. Ithaca: Cornell University Press, 1965.

Hill, Lewis E. "Rates of Return on Municipal Subsidies to Industry: Comment." *Southern Economic Journal* 30 (1964): 358-59.

Hirsch, Werner Z. "Fiscal Impact of Industrialization on Local Schools." *Review of Economics and Statistics* 46 (1964): 191-99.

Hoover, Edgar M. *The Location of Economic Activity*. New York: McGraw-Hill, 1948.

_____. *Location Theory and the Shoe and Leather Industry*. Cambridge: Harvard University Press, 1937.

Hopkinson, R. "Government Financial Assistance for Industrial Development in Canada." *Conference Board Record* 5 (1968): 20-24.

Howard, Dick, and Jerrold L. Stark. "Evaluating Industrial Development Promotion Programs." *American Industrial Development Council Journal* 5 (1970): 33-44.

"Industrial Aid Bonds." *Federal Reserve Bank of Richmond, Monthly Review*, January 1967, 8-11.

"Industrial Bond Controversy Boils." *National Civic Review* 53 (1964): 329-30.

"1970 Industrial Research Guide to State Assistance to Industry." *Industrial Research* 12 (1970): 55-57.

"Industry's Hidden Dividends." *Nation's Business* 58 (1970): 74-90.

Isard, Walter. *Methods of Regional Analysis: An Introduction to Regional Science*. Cambridge: MIT-Press, 1960.

Johnson, William A. "Industrial Tax Exemptions: Sound Investment or Foolish Giveaway?" In *Proceedings of the 55th Annual Conference on Taxation*, National Tax Association. 1962.

Jorgenson, Dale W. "Econometric Studies of Investment Behavior: A Survey." *Journal of Economic Literature* 9 (1971): 1111-47.

———. "The Theory of Investment Behavior." In *Determinants of Investment Behavior*, edited by Robert Gerber. New York: National Bureau of Economic Research, 1967.

Julian, R. "New Look in Industrial Financing." *Industrial Development* 139 (1970): 9-11.

Karaska, G.J., and D.F. Bramhall, eds. *Locational Analysis for Manufacturing*. Cambridge: MIT Press, 1969.

Kee, W.S. "Industrial Development and Its Impact on Local Finance." *Quarterly Review of Economics and Business* 8 (1968): 19-24.

Kentucky Department of Commerce. *The Tax Climate in Kentucky*. Frankfort, 1967.

Kimball, Ralph C. "States as Financial Intermediaries." *New England Economic Review*, January-February 1976, 17-29.

Kinnard, William N., Jr., and Stephen D. Messner. *Industrial Real Estate*. Washington, D.C.: Society of Industrial Realtors, 1973.

Laird, W.E., and J.R. Rinehart. "Neglected Aspects of Industrial Subsidy." *Land Economics* 43 (1967): 25-31.

Lane, Theodore. "The Urban Base Multiplier: An Evaluation of the State of the Art." *Land Economics* 42 (1966): 339-48.

Lamphier, Charles E. *Industrial Development Bond Financing in Action*. Thesis, Stonier Graduate School of Banking, American Bankers Association, New Brunswick, 1964.

Laughlin, Thomas C. "Industrial Development Financing: Mississippi Plan for Progress." *Public Administration Survey* 15 (1967): 1-6.

Levin, Sharon G. "Suburban-Central City Property Tax Differentials and the Location of Industry: Some Evidence." *Land Economics* 50 (1974): 380-86.

"Lining Up to Battle over Industrial Bonds." *Business Week*, March 16, 1968, 136.

Liston, Linda. "Air and Water Pollution: Does It Limit Industrial Expansion?" *Industrial Development and Manufacturers Record* 136 (1967): 14-20.

_____. "States Legislate Generous Remedies for Adverse Business Environment," *Industrial Development* 138 (1969): 2-13.

Loewenstein, Louis K. "The Impact of New Industry on the Fiscal Revenues and Expenditures of Suburban Communities." *National Tax Journal* 16 (1963): 113-36.

McCollom, William C. "Industrial Development Bonds and Tax Policy: A Trend Toward Vivisection of Public Finance." *The Tax Lawyer* 23 (1970): 383-97.

McLaughlin, Glen E., and Stefan Robock. *Why Industry Moves South*. Washington, D.C.: National Planning Association, 1949.

McLure, Charles E., Jr. "Taxation, Substitution and Industrial Location." *Journal of Political Economy* 78 (1970): 112-32.

McMillen, T.E., Jr. "Why Manufacturers Choose Plant Locations vs. Determinants of Plant Locations." *Land Economics* 41 (1965): 239-46.

Marcus, Matityahu, and Daryl Hellman. "The Temporary Stability of Localization Quotients: An Empirical Evaluation." *Economic and Business Bulletin* 22 (1970): 11-17.

Marglin, Stephen. "Economic Factors Effecting System Design." In *Design of Water Resource Systems*, edited by Arthur Maass et al. Cambridge: Harvard University Press, 1962.

_____. "Objectives of Water Resource Development: A General Statement." In *Design of Water-Resource Systems*, edited by Maass et al. Cambridge: Harvard University Press, 1962.

_____. "The Opportunity Cost of Public Investment." *Quarterly Journal of Economics* 77 (1963): 274-89.

Maryland Department of Economic Development. *Digest of Maryland Taxes and Fees, July 1970-June 1971*. Annapolis, n.d.

_____. *Industrial Financing in Maryland*. Annapolis, 1970.

_____. *Maryland Basic Plant Location Data*. Annapolis, 1970.

_____. *Maryland . . . R&D Country*. Annapolis, 1968.

Maryland, Laws of. "Industrial Buildings for Counties and Municipalities." (Revenue Bond Law) Article 41, Sect. 266A-266I, 1970.

_____. "Maryland Industrial Development Financing Authority Law." Article 41, Sect. 266J-266CC. Annapolis, 1970.

Massachusetts Department of Commerce and Development. *A Guide to Massachusetts Industrial Development Financing Programs*. Boston, 1970.

_____. "Procedures for Implementation of the Industrial Bond Statute." Chapter 722 of Acts of 1967. Boston, 1967.

_____. "Regulations for Filing Applications for Certificate of Convenience and Necessity for Industrial Development Projects." Boston, n.d.

Massachusetts Law. "An Act Providing for a Credit Under the Corporation Excise Law for New or Expanded Investment in Massachusetts by Manufacturing or Research and Development Corporations, and Corporations Primarily Engaged in Agriculture or Commercial Fishing." Chapter 634. Boston, 1970.

_____. "An Act Providing Financial Assistance for a Water Pollution Abatement Program for Industrial Wastes." Chapter 746. Boston, n.d.

_____. "An Act Providing for Further Industrial Development of Cities and Towns." Chapter 772. Boston, 1967.

Massachusetts Legislative Research Council. *Report Relative to State Loans to Local Industrial Development Commissions*. House No. 3023. Boston, 1961.

Massachusetts Senate Bill No. 271, 1970. "A Bill Amending Chapter 40D, Sect. 1, Paragraph K, and Chapter 40D, Sect. 1, Paragraph L." Boston, n.d.

May, William L., Jr. "Industrial Bonds: Local Industrial Development Bond Financing." *Boston College Industrial and Commercial Law Review* 7 (1966): 696-705.

Merrill, Kenneth E., and David L. Ryther. *Plant Location and Community Changes*. Lawrence: Center for Research in Business, University of Kansas, 1961.

Meyer, Charles R. "Tax Aspects of Lease Transactions." *The Tax Executive* 23 (1971): 616-50.

Mieszkowski, Peter M. "On the Theory of Tax Incidence." *Journal of Political Economy* 75 (1967): 250-62.

Miller, Ernest G. *Municipal Financial Inducements to Industry: Policy Consequences*. Occasional Paper Series No. 3. Davis: Institute of Governmental Affairs, University of California, 1964.

Miller, Merton H., and Franco Modigliani. "Dividend Policy, Growth, and the Valuation of Shares." *Journal of Business* 34 (1961): 411-33.

_____. "Some Estimates of the Cost of Capital to the Electric Utility Industry, 1954-57." *American Economic Review* 56 (1966): 333-91.

Miller, Richard B. *Plant Location Factors, United States: 1966*. Plant Location Study No. 4. Park Ridge, N.J.: Noyes Development Corporation, 1966.

Mishan, E.J. "The Postwar Literature on Externalities: An Interpretive Essay." *Journal of Economic Literature* 9 (1971): 1-28.

Mitchell, John N. "Municipal Industrial Aid Bonds." *Municipal Finance* 33 (1961): 163-68.

Modigliani, Franco, and Merton H. Miller. "Corporate Income Taxes and the Cost of Capital: A Correction." *American Economic Review* 53 (1963): 433-43.

_____. "The Cost of Capital, Corporation Finance and the Theory of Investment." *American Economic Review* 48 (1958): 261-96.

_____. "The Cost of Capital, Corporation Finance, and the Theory of Investment: Reply." *American Economic Review* 49 (1959): 655-69.

Moes, John E. *Local Subsidies for Industry*, Chapel Hill: University of North Carolina Press, 1962.

_____. "Local Subsidies for Industry: Reply." *Southern Economic Journal* 29 (1962): 119-26.

_____. "The Subsidization of Industry by Local Communities in the South." *Southern Economic Journal* 28 (1961): 187-93.

"More Opinion Noted on Industrial Aid Bonds." *National Civic Review* 61 (1967): 476-77.

Morgan, William E. "The Effects of State and Local Tax and Financial Inducements on Industrial Location." Ph.D. dissertation, University of Colorado, 1964.

Morss, Elliott R. "The Potentials of Competitive Subsidization." *Land Economics* 62 (1966): 161-69.

Mueller, Eva, and James N. Morgan. "Location Decisions of Manufacturers." *American Economic Review* 52 (1962): 204-17.

Munzenrider, Robert F. "Financing Industrial Development: Local

Financing of Industrial Development in Georgia." *Georgia Business* 27 (1967): 6-9.

Nash, J.M. "Case for Industrial Revenue Bond Financing." *Commercial and Financial Chronicle* 207 (1968): 2150.

National Tax Association Property Tax Committee. "The Erosion of the Ad Valorem Real Estate Tax Base." *Tax Policy* 40 (1973): 1-94.

Nebel, Eddystone C. III. *Factors Affecting the Location of the Petrochemical Industry in the Gulf South.* New Orleans: Louisiana State University, 1971.

Nelson, David H. "Tax Considerations of Municipal Industrial Incentive Financing." *Taxes* 45 (1967): 941-48.

New Jersey Department of Conservation and Economic Development. *The Impact of Population and Economic Growth on the Environment of New Jersey.* Trenton, 1965.

———. *Supply and Demand Factors of Industrial Land Use.* Trenton, 1963.

New York Job Development Authority. *Annual Report.* Albany, 1970.

———. New York Job Development Act with Pertinent Extracts from the New York State Constitution. Albany, n.d.

———. *New York Job Development Authority Summary of Loans Approved, January 25, 1962 to March 31, 1970.* Albany: Department of Commerce, 1970.

New York State Department of Commerce. *Urban Tax Incentives in New York State.* Albany: Urban Job Incentive Board, n.d.

———. *The Use of Public Funds or Credit in Industrial Location.* Albany, 1974.

New York State Urban Development Corporation. *New York State Urban Development Act of 1968.* Albany, 1968.

1974 U.S. Master Tax Guide. Chicago: Commerce Clearing House, 1973.

North, Douglass C. "Location Theory and Regional Economic Growth." *Journal of Political Economy* 63 (1955): 243-58.

Nourse, Hugh O. *Regional Economics.* New York: McGraw-Hill, 1968.

Oakland, William H. "Local Taxes and Intra-Urban Industrial Location: A Survey." Paper presented at a symposium in Madison, Wisconsin sponsored by the Committee on Taxation, Resources and Economic Development, 1974.

Ohio Tax Study Committee. *Tax Revision Alternatives for the Tax Systems of Ohio*. Columbus, 1962.

Oldman, Oliver, and Henry Aaron. "Assessment-Sales Ratios under the Boston Property Tax." *National Tax Journal* 18 (1965): 36-49.

Pennsylvania Department of Commerce. *Annual Summary of Mortgage Loans*. 1969.

_____. *Industrial Development Projects Announced in Pennsylvania, 1970*.

_____. *Industrial Revenue Bonds and Mortgages Annual Summary of Loans, 1970—no. 2*.

_____. *The Pennsylvania Industrial Development Authority Act*. Harrisburg: The Pennsylvania Redevelopment Area Economic Cooperation and Implementation Act, 1970.

_____. *Pennsylvania Industrial Revenue Bonds and Mortgages, The Industrial Development Authority Law*. Harrisburg, 1970.

_____. *Statistics of Manufacturing Industries, 1967, 1968, 1969*.

Pennsylvania Industrial Development Authority. *Summary of Loan Activities, 1956-1965*. Report No. 28. Harrisburg, 1970.

_____. *Summary of Loans, July 1968-June 1969*. No. 27. Harrisburg, 1969.

Perloff, H.S.; E.S. Dunn, Jr.; E.E. Lampard; and R.F. Muth. *Regions, Resources and Economic Growth*. Baltimore: Johns Hopkins Press, 1960.

Petshek, K.R. "Can Industrial Development Be Systematically Approached? (Philadelphia)." *Land Economics* 44 (1968): 255-68.

Platt, John P. "Industrial Aid Bonds: A Survey of Problems in Their Use." *Arizona Business Bulletin* (1965): 3-6.

Prentice-Hall, Inc. *The Prentice-Hall Guide to State Industrial Development Incentives*. Information Special Report. Englewood Cliffs, N.J., 1963.

Prest, A.R., and R. Turvey. "Cost-Benefit Analysis: A Survey." *The Economic Journal* 75 (1965): 683-735.

Preston, Albert G., Jr. "What State and Local Taxes Mean to

Business." In Tax Institute of America, *State and Local Taxes on Business. Symposium . . . October 1964*. Princeton, N.J., 1965.

Public Affairs Research Council of Louisiana. *Factors Affecting Louisiana Industrial Development*. Baton Rouge, 1962.

"Public Bonds for Private Industry." *PAR Analysis* (1964): 1-10.

"The 'Public Purpose' of Municipal Financing for Industrial Development." *Yale Law Journal* 70 (1961): 789-803.

Rainey, Ronald I. "A Description and Analysis of the Primary Features of Louisiana's Industry Inducement Program." Master's thesis, Louisiana State University, 1967.

Reeves, H. Clyde. "A Case for Industrial Revenue Bonds." In Tax Institute of America, *State and Local Taxes on Business. Symposium . . . October 1964*. Princeton, N.J., 1965.

Rhode Island Development Council. *Customerized Plant Location Service*. Rhode Island Development Council. Providence, n.d.

_____. *General Laws of Rhode Island*. 1956 Title 42. Chapter 26 as Amended by Chapter 197. Providence, 1968.

_____. *Rhode Island Builds for Tomorrow*. Providence, 1969.

Rhode Island Industrial Building Authority. *Annual Report, 1969*. Providence, 1969.

_____. *Rhode Island Guaranteed Mortgage Financing Plan for Industrial Buildings and Machinery and Equipment*. Providence, n.d.

Richardson, Harry W. *Regional Economics*. New York: Praeger, 1969.

Rinehart, James R. "Rates of Return on Municipal Subsidies to Industry." *Southern Economic Journal* 29 (1963): 297-306.

_____. "Rates of Return on Municipal Subsidies to Industry: Reply." *Southern Economic Journal* 30 (1964): 359-61.

_____, and William E. Laird. "Community Inducements to Industry and the Zero-Sum Game." *Scottish Journal of Political Economy* 19 (1972): 73-90.

Ritter, C. Willis. "Federal Income Tax Treatment of Municipal Obligations: Industrial Development Bonds." *The Tax Lawyer* 25 (1972): 511-36.

Rose, Joseph R. "The Cost of Capital, Corporation Finance and the Theory of Investment: Comment." *American Economic Review* 49 (1959): 638-39.

Rose, Robert E., and Hodde, C.W. *Industrial Tax Loads in Washington and Competing States: a Four Industry Tax Cost Comparison.* (A Joint Study by U.S. Department of Commerce, Economic Development Administration and Washington State Tax Commission. Olympia: Washington State Tax Commission, 1963.

Ross, William D. "Louisiana's Industrial Tax Exemption Program." *Louisiana Business Bulletin* 15 (1953): 20-21.

_____. "Tax Concessions and Their Effect." *Proceedings of the 50th Annual Conference on Taxation.* National Tax Association, 1957.

"The Row over Municipal Industrials." *Fortune* 77 (1968): 191-92.

Sacks, Seymour. "State and Local Finances and Economic Development." In Tax Institute of America, *State and Local Taxes on Business. Symposium . . . October 1964.* Princeton, N.J., 1965.

Samuelson, Paul A. "Tax Deductibility of Economic Depreciation to Insure Invariant Valuations." *Journal of Political Economy* 72 (1964): 604-606.

Sazama, Gerald W. "A Benefit-Cost Analysis of a Regional Development Incentive: State Loans." *Journal of Regional Science* 10 (1970): 385-96.

_____. "State Government Industrial Loan Programs." Ph.D. dissertation, University of Wisconsin, 1967.

_____. "State Industrial Development Loans." *Land Economics* 46 (1970): 171-80.

Schmenner, Roger W. "City Taxes and Industry Location." Ph.D. dissertation, Yale University, 1973.

Schriver, William R. "The Industrialization of the Southeast Since 1950: Some Causes of Manufacturing Relocation with Speculation About Its Effects." *American Journal of Economics and Sociology* 30 (1971): 47-69.

Securities Industry Association (formerly Investment Bankers' Association). *Municipal Statistical Bulletin*, various issues.

Segal, Martin. *Wages in the Metropolis: Their Influence on the Location of Industries in the New York Region.* Cambridge: Harvard University Press, 1960.

Seligman, Bernard. "Use of Public Credit for Private Business

Through Bond Issues." *Financial Analysts Journal* 22 (1966): 141-43.

Sen, A.K. "On Optimizing the Rate of Saving." *Economic Journal* 71 (1961): 479-96.

Shaw, Robert B. "The Advantages and Disadvantages in Tax-Exempts." *Magazine of Wall Street* 113 (1963): 320-322.

Sherman, Roger, and Thomas D. Willett. "Regional Development, Externalities and Tax-Subsidy Combinations." *National Tax Journal* 22 (1969): 291-93.

Sinclair, Stanley. "Gimmick?—or Good Business?" *Financial World* 121 (1964): 20.

Singhvi, S.S., and J.G. Slamka. "Industrial Revenue Bonds: A Source of Long-Term Financing." *California Management Review* 11 (1969): 53-60.

Smith, Theodore Reynolds. *Real Property Taxation and the Urban Center*. Hartford: John C. Lincoln Institute, 1972.

Sosnick, Stephen H. *Local Tax Impact of a New Plant*. Occasional Paper Series No. 1. Davis: Institute of Governmental Affairs, University of California, 1964.

Soule, Don M. *Comparative Total Tax Loads of Selected Manufacturing Corporations with Alternative Locations in Kentucky, Indiana, Ohio, and Tennessee*. Lexington: University of Kentucky, 1960.

"States Push for Industrial Incentives." *Industrial Development* 138 (1969): 17.

Steiner, Peter O. "Choosing Among Alternative Public Investments in the Water Resource Field." *American Economic Review* 49 (1959): 893-916.

Stevens, Benjamin H., and Carolyn A. Brackett. *Industrial Location: A Review and Annotated Bibliography of Theoretical, Empirical and Case Studies*. Philadelphia: Regional Science Research Institute, 1967.

———, and Robert E. Coughlin. *An Investigation of Location Factors Influencing the Economy of the Philadelphia Region*. Regional Science Research Institute Paper No. 12. Philadelphia, 1967.

Stinson, Thomas F. *Financing Industrial Development Through State and Local Governments*. Agricultural Economic Report

No. 128. Economic Research Service, U.S. Department of Agriculture. Washington, D.C. 1967.

Stober, William J. *Taxes, Subsidies and Locational Choice*. Program on the Role of Growth Centers in Regional Economic Development. Discussion Paper No. 36. Lexington: University of Kentucky, 1970.

_____, and Laurence H. Falk. "A Benefit-Cost Analysis of Local Water Supply." *Land Economics* 43 (1967): 328-35.

_____. "The Effect of Financial Inducements on the Location of Firms." *Southern Economic Journal* 36 (1969): 25-35.

_____. "Evaluating Investment Decisions of State and Local Governments." *Growth and Change* 1 (1970): 38-42.

_____. "Industrial Development Bonds as a Subsidy to Industry." *National Tax Journal* 22 (1969): 232-43.

_____. "Poorly Conceived Financial Inducements: A Study of Louisiana's Gas Severance Tax Rebate." *Social Science Quarterly* 51 (1970): 108-19.

_____. "Property Tax Exemption: An Efficient Subsidy to Industry." *National Tax Journal* 20 (1967): 386-94.

_____. "State and Local Inducements to Industrial Development." Paper presented at the 38th Conference of the Southern Economic Association, Washington, D.C., 1968.

_____, and Robert B. Ekelund. "Cost Bias in Benefit-Cost Analysis: Comment." *The Southern Economic Journal* 34 (1968): 563-68.

Tax Foundation. "Financial Inducements to Industrial Location." *Tax Review* 21 (1960): 5-8.

"A Tax Incentive That's Coming Under Fire." *U.S. News & World Report* (January 12, 1967): 94-96.

Taylor, Milton C. *Industrial Tax-Exemption in Puerto Rico: A Case Study in the Use of Tax Subsidies for Industrializing Under-Developed Areas*. Madison: University of Wisconsin, 1957.

Thompson, Arthur A. "Social Benefits of Tax-Exempt Industrial Development Bonds." *Financial Analysts Journal* 24 (1968): 99-103.

Thompson, James H. "Local Subsidies for Industry: Comment." *Southern Economic Journal* 29 (1962): 114-19.

Thompson, Wilbur R., and John M. Mattila. *An Econometric Model of Post-War State Industrial Development*. Detroit: Wayne State University Press, 1959.

Tilden, Robert J. "Public Inducements for Industrial Location: Lesson for Massachusetts." *Maine Law Review* 18 (1966): 1-24.

U.S. Bureau of the Budget. Office of Statistical Standards. *Standard Industrial Classification Manual*. Washington, D.C.: U.S. Government Printing Office, 1967.

U.S. Bureau of the Census. *Annual Survey of Manufactures*. Washington, D.C.: U.S. Government Printing Office, various years.

_____. *Census of Governments*. Vol. 2: *Taxable Property Values and Assessment—Sales Price Ratios and Tax Rates*. Washington, D.C.: U.S. Government Printing Office, 1968 and 1973.

_____. *Census of Manufactures*. Washington, D.C.: U.S. Government Printing Office, various years.

_____. *County Business Patterns, U.S. Summary CPB*. Washington, D.C.: U.S. Government Printing Office, various years.

U.S. Congress. Senate Subcommittee on Intergovernmental Relations of the Committee on Government Operations. *Status of Property Tax Administration in the States*. 93d Cong., 1st sess., March 23, 1973.

U.S. Department of Commerce. *Survey of Current Business*. Washington, D.C.: U.S. Government Printing Office, various issues.

_____. Economic Development Administration. *Industrial Location as a Factor in Regional Economic Development*. Prepared for the Office of Regional Development Planning by Management and Economic Research Incorporated. Washington, D.C.: U.S. Government Printing Office, 1967.

U.S. Office of Business Economics. *Growth Patterns in Employment by County, 1940-50 and 1950-60*. Washington, D.C.: U.S. Government Printing Office, 1965.

Walker, Mabel. "Fiscal Considerations Involved in Patterns of Industrial Development." *Tax Policy* 31 (1964): 3-8.

_____. "Some Tax Factors in Industrial Location." *Tax Policy* 30 (1963): 2-8.

Weiss, Steven J. "Tax Structure, Tax Competition and Tax Burdens on Industry, Part I." *New England Business Review* 1968, 2-12.

Welsh, Richard, and Ruth Brownell. *Potential Tax and Other Incentives for the Economic Development of the State of Hawaii.* Honolulu: Hawaii Department of Planning and Economic Development, 1966.

Wightman, James W. *The Impact of State and Local Fiscal Policies on Redevelopment Areas in the Northeast.* Research Report No. 40. Boston: Federal Reserve Bank of Boston, 1968.

Williams, William V. "A Measure of the Impact of State and Local Taxes on Industry Location." *Journal of Regional Science* 7 (1967): 49-59.

Williamson, R.B. "Some Evidence in Support of State Industrial Financing Programs: The Southwestern Case." *Land Economics* 44 (1968): 388-93.

Wonnacott, Ronald J. *Manufacturing Costs and the Comparative Advantages of United States Regions.* Study Paper No. 9. Minneapolis: Upper Midwest Economic Study, University of Minnesota, 1963.

Index

About the Authors

Daryl A. Hellman received the Bachelor of Science degree in Business Administration from Bucknell University, and the Ph.D. in Economics from Rutgers University. She is Associate Professor of Economics at Northeastern University. Her teaching and research interests include urban and regional economics and the economics of crime. Dr. Hellman is the author of numerous journal articles.

Gregory H. Wassall received the Bachelor of Science degree in Industrial Management from Rensselaer Polytechnic Institute and is completing the Ph.D. in Economics at Rutgers University. He is Assistant Professor of Economics at the University of Hartford. He has authored several articles in the fields of state and local public finance and urban economics.

Laurence H. Falk received his undergraduate degree from the University of Denver and the Ph.D. in Economics from Louisiana State University. He is Assistant Professor of Economics at Rutgers University, and his research interests include economic theory and public finance. Dr. Falk has published numerous articles in these fields.